Intersections:
Where Faith and Life Meet

A Cumberland Presbyterian
Adult Resource
Volume 19, Parables

Discipleship Ministry Team
Ministry Council
Cumberland Presbyterian Church

8207 Traditional Place
Cordova, Tennessee 38016

© 2017 Discipleship Ministry Team

All Rights Reserved. No part of this book may be reproduced or transmitted in any form or by any means, electronic or mechanical, including photocopying, recording, or by any information storage or retrieval system, without permission in writing from the publisher. For information contact Discipleship Ministry Team, Cumberland Presbyterian Center, 8207 Traditional Place, Cordova, Tennessee, 38016-7414.

First Edition 2017

Published by The Discipleship Ministry Team
General Assembly Ministry Council of the Cumberland Presbyterian Church
Cordova, Tennessee

ISBN-10: 1-945929-12-X
ISBN-13: 978-1-945929-12-0

We want to hear from you.
Please send your comments about this resource to
the Discipleship Ministry Team at chm@cumberland.org.

OUR UNITED OUTREACH

Table of Contents

Lesson 1	Sowing Seeds	4
Lesson 2	Show Him no Mercy!	14
Lesson 3	That's not Fair!	23
Lesson 4	Two Sons	32
Lesson 5	Wicked Tenants	42
Lesson 6	Save the Date!	52
Lesson 7	Out of Oil!	62
Lesson 8	Investments that Pay	71
Lesson 9	A Solid Foundation	81
Lesson 10	Eat, Drink, and Be Merry	90
Lesson 11	A Reversal of Fortunes	99
Lesson 12	They Know His Voice	109
Lesson 13	The Kingdom of Heaven Is Like…	119

Unless otherwise specified, all scripture text is from the New Revised Standard Version Bible, copyright 1989, Division of Christian Education of the National Council of the Churches of Christ in the United States of America. Used by permission. All rights reserved.

Editor: Cindy Martin
Proofreaders: Pam Campbell and Marsha Hudson

To order, call 901-276-4572, x 252 or e-mail resources@cumberland.org.

Sowing Seeds

Scripture for lesson: Isaiah 6:9-10;
Matthew 13:1-9, 14-15, 18-23

I have recently been rereading some of the novels I was assigned in high school and listening again to some of the music I studied in college. I have discovered that the books aren't quite like I recalled, and the music doesn't sound the same either. Of course, the books and the music aren't any different; the changes have occurred in me.

Consider a classic story like *Huckleberry Finn* or *To Kill a Mockingbird*, or even a novel such as *1984*. My children are at the ages where these books are assigned reading. I enjoyed these books when I first read them. I understood them in the way that was appropriate for me at that time, given my experience and the context of the world in which I lived. But now I see subtle political messages that before were lost on me in the midst of a good story. I am now aware of conflict in places that previously seemed to be a simple matter of right or wrong.

The same is true in listening to music that I studied years ago. It is even true for the music that was popular during my youth. The subtle dissonances, the interplay of words and melody, the sometimes shocking meaning of lyrics are all evidence that I have changed, not that the music itself has changed.

If I reread those books yet again in another decade, or if I listen to that music again later, they will probably seem different yet again.

Prep for the Journey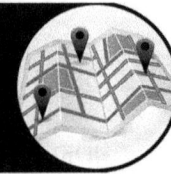

Jesus told many parables. According to *The New Interpreter's Study Bible*, the word *parable* literally means "to throw alongside." Therefore, a parable is a story "thrown out" to illustrate a specific truth. Sometimes, though, the message the teller is trying to convey can be difficult to discern. Jesus' followers seemed to have this problem. As we read, maybe we will also have similar difficulties in agreeing on Jesus' message to the crowd.

What books, music, or other works of art seem different to you now than when you first encountered them? What is the cause of that difference?

In what ways is your understanding different now than it once was? How is it better? worse?

When have you experienced difficulty conveying a message? What devices (drawings, examples, etc.) were ultimately helpful in the successful conveyance of your message?

On the Road

Read Matthew 13:1-9.

That same day Jesus went out of the house and sat beside the sea. ² Such great crowds gathered around him that he got into a boat and sat there, while the whole crowd stood on the beach. ³ And he told them many things in parables, saying: "Listen! A sower went out to sow. ⁴ And as he sowed, some seeds fell on the path, and the birds came and ate them up. ⁵ Other seeds fell on rocky ground, where they did not have much soil, and they sprang up quickly, since they had no depth of soil. ⁶ But when the sun rose, they were scorched; and since they had no root, they withered away. ⁷ Other seeds fell among thorns, and the thorns grew up and choked them. ⁸ Other seeds fell on good soil and brought forth grain, some a hundredfold, some sixty, some thirty. ⁹ Let anyone with ears listen!"

You have probably heard these words many times if you are a longtime churchgoer or someone who has studied the Bible. You likely also have read Jesus' explanation that comes just a few verses later. It is very difficult to set aside any knowledge we have of a scripture so that we can study it, which may keep us from gaining new insights that we weren't quite ready to receive the last time we studied the same words. But perhaps you have heard something new in these words today. Perhaps you are able to hear these words just a little differently than you heard them the last time.

Let's try to examine the meaning of these words as if we haven't heard Jesus' explanation. The crowds weren't able to have Jesus explain this parable to them, so let's try to look at them as if we were in the crowd.

One of the first things that would have come to mind for agricultural people is that this sower was awfully wasteful. It is easy to grasp that seed will not produce if it is sown on a well-worn path, on rocky ground, or in the middle of thorn bushes. Any farmer would know that. The seed was valuable, so the wastefulness would have been quickly noted.

A second thing to note is that of the four places where seed fell, the first three were not productive. If we imagine that equal amounts of seed were spread in each place (something that is not in the text, but that may be imagined by the way the story is told), then we have to realize that three-fourths of the seed that was spread either did not grow at all or was unable to mature to the point of producing a crop. We may wonder what Jesus was trying to say about this farmer or about this method of sowing seed. It would seem to be pretty ineffective.

Finally, the first crowds would have noticed the last part of the parable. The seed that fell on good soil grew one hundredfold, sixty-

> How has your understanding of this parable changed since you first heard it?

> What are some issues in this parable that capture your imagination? Why?

> How difficult or easy is it for you to hear these words without considering Jesus' explanation? How does putting aside Jesus' explanation change the way you view the words? the way you view the crowds and the disciples who didn't understand?

fold, or thirtyfold. Studies about this number are not conclusive. Some sources seem to indicate that seed producing a hundredfold was not unheard of, but those sources don't seem to be from Palestine. Other sources indicate that somewhere between four and tenfold would have been a more reasonable expectation for seed that did well. One hundredfold or even thirtyfold seems to be an almost unattainable number. It possibly references Genesis 26:12, where the mark of Isaac's blessing in a foreign land by God was that he was able to produce at the rate of one hundredfold.

Without considering Jesus' explanation, we can see how people might have been confused by this parable. Even the disciples didn't understand what Jesus was talking about. They had to ask him later.

Scenic Route

After hearing Jesus telling this story, the crowds and the disciples were confused not only about this parable, but about why Jesus used parables at all.

The Gospel of Mark says that Jesus taught in parables specifically so that people to whom the kingdom of God had not been revealed would not be able to understand. (See Mark 4.) Matthew, though, claimed that Jesus' teachings were a fulfillment of the words of Isaiah.

Read Isaiah 6:9-10.
And he said, "Go and say to this people:

*'Keep listening, but do not comprehend;
keep looking, but do not understand.'
¹⁰ Make the mind of this people dull,
   and stop their ears,
   and shut their eyes,
so that they may not look with their eyes,
   and listen with their ears,
and comprehend with their minds,
   and turn and be healed."*

Compare the words of Matthew with those of Isaiah.

> What do you think about the idea of Jesus using parables so that some people would not be able to understand?

Read Matthew 13:14-15.
*With them indeed is fulfilled the prophecy of Isaiah that says:
'You will indeed listen, but never understand,
   and you will indeed look, but never perceive.
¹⁵ For this people's heart has grown dull,
   and their ears are hard of hearing,*

and they have shut their eyes;
so that they might not look with their eyes,
and listen with their ears,
and understand with their heart and turn—
and I would heal them.'

Isaiah and Mark indicate that the people did not understand because God had closed their minds, which means that they were unable to change the situation. According to Matthew, the people had grown dim, losing the ability to see, hear, and understand. In this case the people themselves were to blame.

But the disciples didn't only want to know why Jesus taught in parables. They wanted an explanation of this particular parable, too. So, they asked Jesus exactly what he had meant.

Read Matthew 13:18-23.

"Hear then the parable of the sower. ¹⁹ When anyone hears the word of the kingdom and does not understand it, the evil one comes and snatches away what is sown in the heart; this is what was sown on the path. ²⁰ As for what was sown on rocky ground, this is the one who hears the word and immediately receives it with joy; ²¹ yet such a person has no root, but endures only for a while, and when trouble or persecution arises on account of the word, that person immediately falls away. ²² As for what was sown among thorns, this is the one who hears the word, but the cares of the world and the lure of wealth choke the word, and it yields nothing. ²³ But as for what was sown on good soil, this is the one who hears the word and understands it, who indeed bears fruit and yields, in one case a hundredfold, in another sixty, and in another thirty."

Jesus' explanation helped the people better understand the parable. The sower was spreading the word of the kingdom in every direction. As we read further, we realize that the soil represents human beings in different mindsets or situations. As the seed falls on them, all of them are affected in some way. Jesus may have been saying that when the word is sown, the type of soil isn't immediately apparent. In a group of many people, perhaps one-fourth is like a path, one-fourth is like rocky soil, one-fourth is like thorny ground, and one-fourth is like good soil. The sower continues to sow, in all directions, so that the good soil may receive its share of seed.

However, there is another possibility. Jesus seemed to indicate that the sower was continually sowing the seed. As any farmer or gardener knows, you sow different seeds at different times. For instance, in most areas of the United States, wheat is sown in the fall and harvested in early summer. You plant peas and cabbage before green beans and corn. So it is with people. We are not all ready to receive the seed at the same time. Maybe the thorns or stones need to be removed or the packed dirt of a path broken so that the seeds will be able to take root.

Matthew's change in the quote from Isaiah may enter into the interpretation here. Isaiah suggested that God had closed the eyes and

---

What difference does Matthew's slight deviation from the text of Isaiah make to you? How does it change the meaning of Jesus' teaching about parables? How can we reconcile this word with the Gospel of Mark?

When have you seen people whose responses to the gospel message compare to the types of soil? How have you seen these same people's reactions change over time?

How do you interpret Jesus' continual sowing of seed in all directions?

Whose responsibility is it to continue to sow seeds?

> How can a person's "soil" be changed? How does your faith community help to cultivate the soil to encourage growth?

ears of the people. In other words, God had turned the people into poor soil. But Matthew suggested the people themselves had caused this to happen.

The condition of soil can be changed by adding fertilizer, tilling it, removing rocks, and killing the thorns. When God, Jesus, or the Spirit work with humans to clear their eyes and unstop their ears, the condition of the soil is changed. It takes hard work to clear rocks out of a field, but it can be done. It takes hard work to clear thorny bushes from the ground, but it can be done. It takes hard work to break up and plow a path that has been tread upon and crushed underfoot, but it can be done.

Perhaps the people's goal, perhaps our goal, is to allow God to change us so that we can be the type of ground where the word will grow easily and produce much.

Workers Ahead

It has been almost 2,000 years since Jesus taught the people with this parable, but it still speaks to us today. Many of us have seen people react in the various ways Jesus described. Some of us may recognize ourselves in the story and remember how we reacted the first time the seed of God's love was sown on the soil of our lives.

I am always amazed at the ability of plants to find a way to grow even in difficult circumstances. Perhaps you have seen a rock or a section of concrete that, over time, has been invaded by plants. At first maybe only a small sprout took root, but as that sprout grew, it cracked a boulder or destroyed a sidewalk. This can happen on a worn down path as well, once the path is no longer trampled. All the types of soil about which Jesus talked in the parable can produce fruit in great quantity if the seeds continue to be sown and impediments are removed.

> What type of soil are you? What amounts of fruit are you producing? What are the impediments to your being the good soil that Jesus described? How can you remove those impediments?

What does Jesus parable say to us? Maybe we have become hardened so that the seed cannot penetrate us. Maybe we need to soften our hearts and let the seed do its work of growing within us. Maybe we have rocks in our soil, things that block the seed from taking strong root. Fear, distrust, and doubt often block us from being receptive. Maybe the cares of the world have become so strong in us that we cannot allow in enough light to let the seeds grow. We may need to assess what is choking the light away from the seed of God's kingdom.

In the Rear View

Jesus loved to teach in parables, and those parables are continually being reread and reinterpreted by his followers. This parable may mean something very different to us than it did when we first heard it. Maybe we were like one type of soil at another time in our lives, but have changed due to a willingness to hear and accept God's word. Or maybe things in our lives have made it harder to produce fruit.

Wherever we are right now, we can read the parable of the sower with hope that, through our work and in partnership with God, we can continue to improve our own soil so that we might better produce the fruit of God's kingdom.

How has your "soil" changed? What caused those changes?

Travel Log

Day 1:

Write down your favorite scripture. Why is it your favorite? When did you first hear it? What did it mean to you then? How has its meaning changed for you over the years? Doodle some words around the scripture that indicate what the passage means to you now.

Day 2:

Take a walk or spend some time outside. What do you notice about the beauty of creation? What do you see, hear, and smell? Write down some of those sensations and reflect about how time spent in nature helps you to grow in your faith in God.

Day 3:

Imagine yourself as a person in the crowd when Jesus taught the parable of the sower. Write down some of the questions you might have or some of the observations that you might have drawn from Jesus' teaching that day.

Day 4:

When have you received the word of God but did not understand it (represented by the soil on the path in the parable)? What events have caused you to become downtrodden—perhaps even to the point that God's word could not penetrate your uppermost layers? In the space below write what advice you would give to someone who was like the soil of the path.

Day 5:
Reflect on what it must be like to have rocky soil. What types of "rocks" would keep someone from allowing the word of God to root and grow? List some steps that can be taken to break up or remove those rocks.

Day 6:
Think of your own life. What cares do you have that are choking out your ability to create fruit for the kingdom of God? Try to make an honest list of those things that impede your growth in the kingdom.

Day 7:
    Think of times when you have felt like you were the type of soil that could produce a hundredfold. How can you help make that your permanent identity? List some actions you can take every day to keep yourself ready to grow the kingdom of God.

Show Him no Mercy!

Scripture for Lesson: Matthew 18:21-35

Every week in churches throughout the world, people pray the prayer that Jesus taught his disciples. My congregation prays the Lord's Prayer as part of our worship service every time we meet. However, the message of that prayer can lose some of its impact simply because we use it so often that we don't always think about its content.

There is a line in the prayer that varies from church to church. In my congregation we say, "And forgive us our debts as we forgive our debtors...." In the church where I grew up, we used the word *trespasses*. Other churches may use the word sins or even something else.

It is quite a request that we make to God in this moment of worship. We are asking God to forgive us in the way that we forgive others. If we really mean these words, we should see just how important it is for us to be forgiving. Implicit within the request is that if we are not forgiving to others, God should not be forgiving to us. Scary, huh?

Prep for the Journey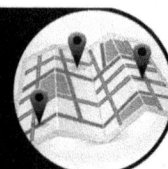

Just a word on how I am choosing to use scripture in this lesson: When studying the Gospels, biblical scholars try to differentiate between which words Jesus spoke and those that were added as interpretation by the writers. Most biblical scholars think that the last verse in the parable for this lesson was added by Matthew, which gives an allegorical interpretation of the parable. Viewing the king as God has some difficult complications. We will be looking at the parable both as the king representing God and as the king representing the ways of the world. Perhaps we can come to appreciate the parable as both.

How much thought do you give to what you are saying when you pray the Lord's Prayer? What would help you to be more intentional about praying the Lord's Prayer rather than reciting it?

How does it feel to know that God holds us to such high standards?

How is it possible to read the same scripture in different ways? What would make it difficult to separate Jesus' words from Matthew's interpretation of them? What are the rewards or the dangers of this type of interpretation?

On the Road

Slavery was an acceptable part of society during Jesus' time. Other than through captivity or other acts of war, there were three primary "ways by which a Jew might become a slave. Sometimes a person would sell himself into service because of debt or extreme poverty. In other instances a person might become a slave in order to make restitution as a convicted thief. A less common event was when a father sold his young daughter into domestic service to another Jew. The intent was that she would marry into the family when she came of age. On her twelfth birthday she returned to her father's home if a marriage had not taken place, as no Jew could own an adult Jewess" (*The Land and People Jesus Knew*, by J. Robert Teringo, ©1985, page 235).

Read Matthew 18:23-35.

"For this reason the kingdom of heaven may be compared to a king who wished to settle accounts with his slaves. ²⁴ When he began the reckoning, one who owed him ten thousand talents was brought to him; ²⁵ and, as he could not pay, his lord ordered him to be sold, together with his wife and children and all his possessions, and payment to be made. ²⁶ So the slave fell on his knees before him, saying, 'Have patience with me, and I will pay you everything.' ²⁷ And out of pity for him, the lord of that slave released him and forgave him the debt. ²⁸ But that same slave, as he went out, came upon one of his fellow slaves who owed him a hundred denarii; and seizing him by the throat, he said, 'Pay what you owe.' ²⁹ Then his fellow slave fell down and pleaded with him, 'Have patience with me, and I will pay you.' ³⁰ But he refused; then he went and threw him into prison until he would pay the debt. ³¹ When his fellow slaves saw what had happened, they were greatly distressed, and they went and reported to their lord all that had taken place. ³² Then his lord summoned him and said to him, 'You wicked slave! I forgave you all that debt because you pleaded with me. ³³ Should you not have had mercy on your fellow slave, as I had mercy on you?' ³⁴ And in anger his lord handed him over to be tortured until he would pay his entire debt. ³⁵ So my heavenly Father will also do to every one of you, if you do not forgive your brother or sister from your heart."

In this section, we will examine the parable using Matthew's interpretation, which indicated that the king, or later the lord, was the representative of God. One of a king's slaves owed him an excessive amount of money. When the slave begged for more time, the king forgave the debt. As the slave was leaving his meeting with the king, he saw a fellow slave who owed him money—but only a pittance when compared to what he had owed the king. Rather than forgive the debt, the first slave demanded immediate repayment. When the

---

Conditions in some parts of the world still cause some families to sell their children. Others are forced into various types of slavery due to economic conditions. How does your faith community address such issues?

How do you react when someone owes you money? How does the amount of money owed affect your reaction?

second slave could not repay the debt, the first slave demanded that he be thrown into prison until the debt was repaid. Upon hearing about the first slave's actions, the king rescinded his forgiveness and punished his slave severely. The degree of punishment was as excessive as had been his earlier forgiveness.

A talent was a measure of money equal to more than fifteen years' wages for a common laborer. Ten thousand talents, then, was worth more than 150 years of a laborer's income. The debt that the slave owed the king was enormous, beyond our ability to fathom. In fact, a talent was the largest denomination of currency, and 10,000 was the largest possible number in the Greek system of numbers. *Talent* literally means "myriad." This enormous sum is something that no one could have repaid, even if given a lifetime to do so. The forgiveness of this type of debt was an act of exceptional grace.

The amount that the second slave owed the first slave was not an insignificant amount either. A *denarius* was the daily wage for a laborer, so 100 *denarii* would have equaled the wages of a laborer for 100 days. I don't know about you, but it would be difficult for me to come up with money equal to 100 working days of wages.

Perhaps the point is the glaring difference between these two amounts. On the one hand, the slave was forgiven an amount that would have been impossible for him to repay. On the other, even having been forgiven his own huge debt, he sent a peer to prison for a relatively small debt.

The king was enraged. Perhaps he was angry because he looked weak in comparison to his own slave. Perhaps he had a sense of justice regarding what this man should have done as a result of his own debt forgiveness. Either way, the king punished the first slave by having him tortured until he was able to repay the debt. In Matthew's version, where the king represents God, this sounds like an eternity of torment, since the debt could never be repaid, especially by a man who had been sentenced to prison and torture.

Scenic Route

There are reasons to interpret this story differently than Matthew presented it. Many biblical scholars practice literary criticism of scripture. They point out that the Gospels, among other literature of the Bible, were not written as a value-neutral historical account, but as statements of faith and persuasion intended to cause others to adopt the beliefs of the writers. Those who study the Gospels also point out that many of the stories and issues in the Gospels reflect the conflicts that were taking place when they were written—at least as much as

---

What parallels/differences can you find between this situation and modern lending practices?

When have you seen forgiveness practiced well? When have you seen people who were unwilling to forgive? What resulted from the lack of forgiveness?

What new insights do you have after reading this parable again? What information is surprising? What is disturbing?

the conflicts in Jesus' time. The Gospel of Matthew was finally preserved in written form many years after Jesus' death and resurrection.

The words of the Gospel, even sometimes the way the words of Jesus were written, could reflect a bias on the part of the writer. Take, for instance, this parable. The last two verses, 34-35, may have been Matthew's way of making a point with Jesus' words. Scholars have especially questioned verse 35 as being the only way to interpret Jesus' story.

How does the idea that the Gospel writers may have added their own biases affect your understanding of scripture?

There are many indications that suggest the king in the parable is nothing like God. It is likely that if Jesus were trying to present a king who was like God, that king would have adhered to Jewish principles of fairness and Jewish Law in his edicts. The king, however, seems to have a lot of Gentile traits. First, the amount of money involved is far above any amount that would have been available to a Jewish ruler. Second, the servant, when asking for forgiveness, bowed down and worshiped the king, something a Jew would not have been allowed to do. Third, Jewish Law prohibited the wife of a family from being sold into slavery. And fourth, Jewish Law allowed for imprisonment for debt, but not torture (*The New Interpreter's Bible, Vol. VIII*, © 1995, page 381). The king was very different from what one would have expected a righteous, Jewish ruler to be.

What do you think about the idea that the king in this story is not meant to represent God? How does that change the way you understand the parable?

There is also the problem of a king taking back forgiveness that had already been offered. Theologically, that is a difficult message about God. Some might argue that the slave had never actually received forgiveness because he had been unwilling to offer it, but the granting of forgiveness was not conditional at the beginning of the story. In other words, the picture of the king in this story, while being forgiving at first, is of a Gentile king who lorded power over others. In trying to be tougher than his own slave, he required a harsh punishment for a debt that had already been forgiven. In that case, the story may be an example of how awful the world is when people do not forgive as God forgives.

Does the choice of how to accept the presentation of the king in this parable make a difference in the way you perceive God? Why or why not?

Workers Ahead

Just before Jesus told this parable, he and Peter had had a conversation about forgiveness. Maybe the key to understanding how this parable applies to us is to look back at that exchange.

Read Matthew 18:21-22.
Then Peter came and said to him, "Lord, if another member of the church sins against me, how often should I forgive? As many as seven times?" 22 Jesus said to him, "Not seven times, but, I tell you, seventy-seven times.

What do Jesus' words about forgiving someone 77 times mean to you?

> What does it mean to forgive? What are the parameters that must be met in order for us to forgive?

The only qualifier in Peter's question is that the offender is a member of the church, or maybe the translation is better understood as "a brother [or sister]." There is no mention of an apology or restitution—no mention of an act of contrition at all. Jesus simply said that the offended party should forgive.

But, does forgiveness mean that the previous relationship is restored? I don't see that in Jesus' words. If one is abused by someone else, one can forgive without restoring the relationship. Forgiveness does not necessarily mean being vulnerable to that person in the future.

> When have you been offended and unwilling to forgive? What would enable you to forgive?

I want to emphasize that the offender does not have the right simply to tell someone else to offer forgiveness and forget about the offense. If I have offended someone, Jesus may speak to that person about forgiving me, but Jesus may well speak to me about attempting to repair the breach. If I owe someone something, I should repay it. If my offense was something else, I should offer to make restitution. Even though scripture tells others to forgive, it also tells offenders to care faithfully for those they have hurt.

In the Rear View

We have discussed the parable of the unforgiving servant and looked at it in ways that cast the king as a substitute for God and with the king as being very different from God. There are lessons to be learned in either case. Forgiveness can be a difficult and very personal process. While Jesus commanded us to forgive, we don't really have a good sense of what forgiveness should look like because every case is different. Every hurt, every pain, every offense is different, and forgiveness will likely look different in each one.

> When have you hurt another and needed to ask for forgiveness? What were you prepared to do in order to restore your relationship with another?

I would like to look back on the beginning of this lesson, when we discussed the Lord's Prayer. We are asking God to forgive us in the same way that we forgive others. At the very least, that conditional phrase should make us examine our own practices of forgiveness. To me, that is one of the most frightening statements I can make to God, and it gives me a sense of the seriousness with which I must take my own forgiveness of others.

Travel Log

Day 1:
What does forgiveness mean to you? What does it mean for you to forgive someone else? What does it mean for you to be forgiven by someone else? Journal your responses in the space below.

Day 2:
Make a list of the godly and non-godly aspects of the king in this parable. Which list seems to be longer? What does that say about the king? What does it say about your concept of who God is?

Day 3:

Recall an incident from your childhood or youth when someone hurt you, and you ultimately forgave him or her. Maybe it was a deep hurt or maybe it was something simple that was easily forgiven. How did it happen? How did it feel? Draw a picture, write a poem, or otherwise express your feelings about the incident.

Day 4:

Take some time to write about a situation where you have been hurt and you have not been able to forgive the other person. What is keeping you from offering forgiveness? How might thinking of forgiveness in terms other than restoring the previous relationship help? Jot down some ideas.

Day 5:

What do you think Jesus was trying to say by making the sums of money owed so vastly different? Identify a situation when someone was willing to forgive a huge amount, a huge hurt. Then recall another time when someone was unwilling to forgive a small amount or a tiny offense. Write about what these situations mean to you.

Day 6:

We may look to the world of politics for stories of offense and lack of forgiveness, but they can all too often be found within our very families. The hurts in these relationships can be difficult to heal, because the closeness of the relationship makes them especially hurtful. Take a moment and think of people close to you who have hurt you or whom you have hurt. Write their names in the space below. Brainstorm how you might be able to reconnect, perhaps not in the same way as before, but restore some type of relationship.

Day 7:
    Write about someone you have hurt. Perhaps it was accidental, perhaps it was on purpose. Why did you do what you did? What was the outcome? Were you able to ask for forgiveness? What do you think might happen if you asked now?

That's not Fair!

Scripture for lesson: Matthew 20:1-16

"That's not fair!" How many times have we said or heard those words? Parents frequently hear the complaint—loudly. It seems that fairness is always being questioned, whether it is about a game, the type of ice cream, or which room is set aside for each child. Surprisingly, it seems that both (or more) children can claim that the same circumstance is unfair.

We don't really ever get over this fixation on fairness, do we? We might wonder where our children's obsession with being fair comes from, but the most likely source is the adults with whom they interact.

If you think you don't care about fairness, recall a time when someone cut in front of you, when someone else received credit for your efforts, when a job went to someone who seemed to be less qualified, when you had to cancel your plans because of an immediate need at work, etc. Feeling that we are being treated unfairly can be very upsetting. In this lesson's parable, we can likely identify with the laborers who were infuriated because they had worked all day and received the same wage as those who had worked only a short time.

Prep for the Journey

Today's parable is part of a longer section that began in chapter 19 in which Matthew told about Jesus blessing the children. When the disciples attempted to keep the children away from Jesus, he replied that the kingdom of heaven belonged to such as those children.

Then Jesus had an encounter with a rich young man who was described as being one who had kept the Law since his youth. Jesus didn't correct him. In fact, Jesus commended him until the young man asked what he lacked. Jesus told him that he must sell all his possessions and give the money to the poor.

How do you handle a situation in which someone claims he or she has been treated unfairly?

What have you recently experienced that was unfair? How did you deal with the situation?

How might you have reacted to Jesus' statement? Why?

I can imagine this man thinking, That's not fair! I have followed the Law and done everything right all this time. Now you want me to give up everything that I have? As the young man walked away, sad because he had so many possessions, Jesus explained to the disciples that it is impossible for the rich to enter heaven, but it is possible for God to do all things.

There are several themes in these exchanges. First, children were extremely low on the social scale in Jesus' time. If they were present in any situation, they would almost assuredly have been ignored. It would have been logical for Jesus' disciples to assume that Jesus didn't want to waste any of his time on children. Instead, however, Jesus said that the kingdom of heaven belongs to ones such as these. The poor, the ignored, the weakest of society actually are the ones who own the kingdom itself.

Then, this rich young man came along. He was the kind of person with whom many people would have wanted to become acquainted. Having him as a friend would have increased their own social standing. Yet Jesus said that in order for him to be "perfect," he must become poor and follow Jesus. The implications weren't only for Jesus and this one man, but the poor who would benefit by having access to this man's wealth.

Jesus then further explained his point by telling a story about laborers in a vineyard. All these statements point toward Jesus' final conclusion: The first shall be last, and the last shall be first.

> How does knowing the low status of children at that time change your understanding of Jesus welcoming them?
>
> What commonalities do you see between Jesus blessing the children and his encounter with the rich young man? What might he have been teaching through these situations?
>
> What does the phrase the *first shall be last and the last shall be first* mean to you?
>
> Where might a situation similar to the one Jesus used be found today?

On the Road

It would have been a relatively normal situation for a group of day laborers, those without specialized skills, to be gathered in the marketplace in the morning, waiting for someone to hire them to work. It is this situation that Jesus chose to use to teach his followers.

Read Matthew 20:1-8.

"For the kingdom of heaven is like a landowner who went out early in the morning to hire laborers for his vineyard. ² After agreeing with the laborers for the usual daily wage, he sent them into his vineyard. ³ When he went out about nine o'clock, he saw others standing idle in the marketplace; ⁴ and he said to them, 'You also go into the vineyard, and I will pay you whatever is right.' So they went. ⁵ When he went out again about noon and about three o'clock, he did the same. ⁶ And about five o'clock he went out and found others standing around; and he said to them, 'Why are you standing here idle all day?' ⁷ They said to him, 'Because no one has hired us.' He said to them, 'You also go into the

vineyard.' ⁸ When evening came, the owner of the vineyard said to his manager, 'Call the laborers and give them their pay, beginning with the last and then going to the first.'"

The normal daily wage for an unskilled laborer was a *denarius*. Those who were hired early in the morning would have expected this to be their wage for a day's work in the fields. It was only enough for these laborers to maintain a life of subsistence. Meager as it was, it was sufficient to get by.

One can already see the dilemma for laborers who went out but were not hired. If the *denarius* was only enough to afford one's daily bread, then not being hired likely meant that the worker and his family would not be able to eat that day.

There are some aspects of the story that are different from the usual practices. The landowner himself went to the marketplace to hire the laborers. Usually that task would have fallen to the property manager. We know from later in the story that there was a manager; he simply wasn't called upon to do the hiring.

The landowner went to the marketplace several times throughout the day to hire more laborers. When he hired them, he did not offer them a specific wage as he had with the first laborers. He simply said that he would pay them "whatever is right."

Although not explicitly stated, it seems likely that those listening to the story would have assumed that the workers would have been paid according to the amount of time they had worked. That seems fair, doesn't it? Those who worked all day would have expected to receive more than those who worked less. Certainly they would have expected to receive more than those who only worked an hour at the end of the day, right?

Who in your community is barely earning a subsistence wage? What resources does your church offer to people in these circumstances?

Why might the landowner have done the hiring himself? How does that fact affect your understanding of the story?

What would you consider to have been "right" to pay those laborers who were hired later in the day? If you ran a business, how would you divide the wages?

Scenic Route

Jesus set up everyone who was hearing this story to expect a certain outcome. Then he surprised them with something completely different.

Read Matthew 20:9-16.

When those hired about five o'clock came, each of them received the usual daily wage. ¹⁰ Now when the first came, they thought they would receive more; but each of them also received the usual daily wage. ¹¹ And when they received it, they grumbled against the landowner, ¹² saying, 'These last worked only one hour, and you have made them equal to us who have borne the burden of the day and the scorching heat.' ¹³ But he replied to one of them, 'Friend, I am doing you no wrong; did you not agree with me for the usual daily wage? [14] *Take what belongs to you and go; I choose to give to this last the same as I give to you.* [15] *Am I not allowed to do what I choose with what belongs to me? Or are you envious because I am generous?'* [16] *So the last will be first, and the first will be last."*

Our concept of fairness and justice had already fixed in our mind that the landowner was going to pay the laborers a rate that corresponded to the number of hours they had worked. But the "right" pay was the full day's wages, even for those who only worked for one hour. How was this fair? How was it just?

The simple answer is that it wasn't fair or just. It was grace. The landowner chose to be generous in a situation in which it was neither required nor expected. He considered what the laborers needed and fulfilled that need. There was nothing in it for him.

Remember, the day's wage didn't provide enough income for people to be able to save. Without that *denarius* every day, their needs (and those of their family) went unmet. The landowner knew that if he paid any of the workers less than a single day's wage, they would not have been able to feed their families. So, instead of giving them what they had earned, the landowner gave them what they needed.

As we have noted before, this parable is part of a larger story that points out the difference between who society thinks is important and who Jesus thinks is important. I imagine that many different types of day laborers had gathered in the marketplace, all wanting and needing to be hired. I imagine the hirers looking through that group and picking out the ones who appeared to be the most valuable. They wanted to get their money's worth, so they chose the laborers who would be able to do the most work. Over the course of the day, the sick, the wounded, the disabled, and the very young or very old would constantly be overlooked as the fittest were selected. I imagine that each time the landowner went back to the marketplace, the laborers who had yet to be hired seemed less and less fit for a day's work. Maybe some of the laborers could only work for an hour at a time.

The landowner hired these whom society would likely see as the least, and he put them to work. Then he paid them according to what they needed rather than what they earned.

Workers Ahead

It is tempting to go straight to the implications of what Jesus meant by this parable. However, it seems clear to me that Jesus was addressing a problem that either was coming up in the community or one that he suspected would soon arise. Those people who had been

---

Put yourself in the position of the various laborers. How do you feel when you are paid? How do you react to what others are paid? What effect do the landowner's words have on your reaction?

When have you been paid more than you felt you deserved? How did the experience make you feel? How has or might if affect the way you treat someone else?

What do you think of the concept that the landowner paid according to what people needed instead of what they earned? How is that concept like the kingdom of God?

following Jesus might feel that they were entitled to special privileges because they had been with him from the beginning. He wanted his followers to understand that in God's kingdom, all were equal

When we look at the "grumbling" of the workers who were hired first, they didn't actually grumble about their wages. They were angry because the landowner made those who were hired later "equal" to them. Those who were hired first would have been happy with the other laborers being paid a full day's wages, as long as they got more. They had no problem with people receiving rewards for their service, but they felt that they should get a larger reward because they had been working longer.

The kingdom of God doesn't work like that. It isn't about fairness or justice, but about grace. It is about giving people what they need, not what they deserve. Let's face it, in theological terms, if we got what we deserved, none of us would be happy with the outcome. Christian theology teaches that we are all sinners who fall short of what we should be. We cannot earn the reward God has for us no matter how many hours or years we work. The end result, if we attain the kingdom of heaven, is a gift of grace.

Jesus wasn't saying that the life of discipleship is not of value. It isn't as if he suggested that people wait until the last hour to start working and then expect to receive the reward. The work of discipleship is about committing oneself to the work to which God has called us. As soon as we are called, we commit ourselves and we work for the full time we can.

But at the same time, we who may be called earlier in our lives cannot be jealous of those who were called later just because they will receive the same reward. Instead, we should rejoice that we share in that reward with as many others as possible.

In the Rear View

In this parable, we probably have more in common with the earlier hired workers than with Jesus' explanation. It certainly seems unfair not to have paid the first workers more, but Jesus explains that this story tells us what the kingdom of heaven is like. God's kingdom is different from the world in which we live.

Although we can understand and even appreciate the concept, maybe we can only truly understand this parable when we are able to see our reality through the lenses of the kingdom of heaven. As we grow in our own discipleship, we will be able to look through that lens more effectively.

What do about this parable do you find difficult to accept? Why?

The lesson Jesus was teaching runs counter to our culture. How can we live it? How can we have this type of kingdom mindset in our daily lives?

When have you grumbled about the unfairness of sharing a reward with someone?

Travel Log

Day 1:

Recall a recent experience when something seemed unfair to you. How did you react to the situation? In what ways could you have reacted better? Reconsider the situation in light of Jesus' words about the kingdom of heaven. Journal your thoughts.

Day 2:

We live in a society that is based almost completely on being rewarded for our personal value to our company, nation, or society. Write about the concept that the laborers were rewarded according to their need, not according to the value of their labor. How can that concept be a part of our kingdom-view of our own society?

Day 3:

Imagine yourself as the rich young man from the passage that immediately precedes this one in the Gospel of Matthew. Would you have the courage or ability to sell your possessions? Why or why not? Why do you think Jesus told him to do so? Jot down some of the implications of selling your possessions.

Day 4:

Put yourself in the role of one of the laborers who was hired at the beginning of the day. Imagine the conversation you would have had with your family when you went home. Note some of the things you might have said.

Day 5:
    Put yourself in the place of the laborers who were hired at the end of the day. They must have been surprised to receive a full day's wage for their one hour of work. When have you been rewarded or paid beyond what was expected? How did you feel? How did that situation address what you needed?

Day 6:
    Imagine yourself listening to Jesus tell this story. How does it feel when Jesus said that the landowner would pay "whatever is right?" When has a similar promise been made to you? How pleased were you with the fulfillment of that promise? How likely would you be to accept a job under those circumstances?
    Write a prayer for those people who labor but don't earn even a subsistence wage.

Day 7:

It is hard to have the kind of vision that Jesus suggested in this parable. How can we develop a kingdom-based economy instead of a value based economy in our lives? List some of the possibilities as well as the consequences.

Two Sons

Scripture for lesson: Matthew 21:23-32, 45

As a child, I had certain chores that I was supposed to do. Sometimes I would do them without many reminders from my parents, but usually I had to be reminded several times. It is hard to get motivated to do things that you really don't want to do.

I wish I could say that as a child I had performed these chores out of respect for my parents, but often I ended up doing them because my parents just wouldn't leave me alone until I did. We can imagine that the sons in the parable for this lesson also had responsibilities at home, especially if they were grown as the story seems to suggest. It is doubtful that they enjoyed their chores any more than I did. I hope that I have developed a better sense of responsibility, like at least one of the sons in today's story.

> **When have you had a hard time doing something for which you were responsible? What feelings and emotions did you experience?**

Prep for the Journey

This parable is one of three that Jesus told on Monday of what we now think of as Holy Week. In Matthew's version of events, Jesus had triumphantly entered Jerusalem the day before while people shouted, "Hosanna!" and waved palm branches. Once in the city, Jesus entered the Temple and overturned the tables of the money changers. After driving out those who were buying and selling at the Temple, which created an atmosphere that was not conducive to worship and prayer, Jesus then healed many people and received the praise of children.

Jesus left the city to spend the night in Bethany, probably with his friends Mary, Martha, and Lazarus, whose home was only a mile or two away. On Monday Jesus made his way back into Jerusalem, cursing a fig tree on the way, and teaching the disciples about prayer and faith. When he entered the Temple, the chief priests and elders of the people challenged his authority for teaching.

> **Why do you think the chief priests and elders challenged Jesus?**

On the Road

The Jews were under Roman rule during Jesus' life. The Jewish religious leaders had power only because the Romans permitted it. Basically they were in charge of the religious Law, which was why they could not sentence Jesus to death. However, their power was tenuous, dependent upon the Romans' whim. If anything or anyone threatened their power, they were eager to eliminate the problem. Jesus' teachings were causing a lot of dissension among the masses. Because people gathered to listen to Jesus and other known teachers, a public "debate" seemed to be a way to discredit him in front of a large number of people. If the chief priests and elders could discredit him, their positions were safe.

Read Matthew 21:23-27.

*When he entered the temple, the chief priests and the elders of the people came to him as he was teaching, and said, "By what authority are you doing these things, and who gave you this authority?" *²⁴* Jesus said to them, "I will also ask you one question; if you tell me the answer, then I will also tell you by what authority I do these things. *²⁵* Did the baptism of John come from heaven, or was it of human origin?" And they argued with one another, "If we say, 'From heaven,' he will say to us, 'Why then did you not believe him?' *²⁶* But if we say, 'Of human origin,' we are afraid of the crowd; for all regard John as a prophet." *²⁷* So they answered Jesus, "We do not know." And he said to them, "Neither will I tell you by what authority I am doing these things."*

Many biblical scholars have written in recent years about the culture in Jesus' time, which is sometimes referred to as an honor-shame culture. The way for a public figure to gain honor was to look good in public. Looking bad caused shame.

One way a public figure could gain honor was by challenging another public figure. It is, in a strange way, reminiscent of a duel or a showdown in the Old West. This is what the chief priests and the elders of the people were trying to do when they confronted Jesus. If Jesus didn't have a satisfactory answer for them, their influence with the people would go up, and Jesus' influence would go down.

But Jesus countered their question with a question. Apparently they hadn't foreseen this possibility, but they were obligated to answer. Note how the chief priests and the elders argued among themselves about how to answer. It wasn't so much that they wanted to get the answer correct, but that they wanted to answer in a way that would help them to gain honor in the culture. Because they determined neither answer would gain honor, they decided to take the least amount of shame, by their calculations, and admit they did not know the answer.

Where have you seen circumstances similar to the setting of this parable? Why was one person or group challenging the other?

What kinds of things influence public approval of today's leaders? What role does or should the church have in such matters?

How easy is it for you to admit that you do not know the answer to a question? How do you feel when that situation arises?

Jesus knew that they could not answer his question in a way that would satisfy the people, so he won the contest that the chief priests and elders had started. But Jesus wasn't willing to stop there. He challenged them back with a hypothetical question.

Read Matthew 21:28-32, 45.

"What do you think? A man had two sons; he went to the first and said, 'Son, go and work in the vineyard today.' ^{29} He answered, 'I will not'; but later he changed his mind and went. ^{30} The father went to the second and said the same; and he answered, 'I go, sir'; but he did not go. ^{31} Which of the two did the will of his father?" They said, "The first." Jesus said to them, "Truly I tell you, the tax collectors and the prostitutes are going into the kingdom of God ahead of you. ^{32} For John came to you in the way of righteousness and you did not believe him, but the tax collectors and the prostitutes believed him; and even after you saw it, you did not change your minds and believe him."...

When the chief priests and the Pharisees heard his parables, they realized that he was speaking about them.

The answer to the question was evident to all. The chief priests and the elders had no choice but to answer Jesus' question. Obviously the first son had done what his father asked. Even though he first refused, he got up and worked. The second son gave his father the answer that he wanted to hear, but he didn't raise a hand to accomplish what his father had asked.

These two stories are together for a reason. The chief priests and elders realized that Jesus had laid a trap for them, but to leave would have meant shame as much as answering poorly would have. They were like the second son. When asked if they would serve the people, go out and work in the fields, they immediately and said they would. They became educated and accepted high ranking places in their faith, but when God sent messengers, John and then Jesus, they ignored them. God asked them to stand up and do what was right, but instead they stuck to their old ways and supported the status quo.

Those who heard John and repented, the people whom others might have cataloged as the worst of sinners, had originally said no to God's calling. Yet when they heard John and then Jesus, they repented and were baptized. They were like the first son, the one who did what the father asked.

When (if ever) have you been in what seemed to be a competition for shame or honor? Where have you seen that type of situation played out in the world? What is it like? How is it possible to remove yourself from that type of system?

What do you think caused the chief priests and the elders to realize that Jesus had been talking about them? Why might they have believed they were the ones serving God and not the other way around? How might you react if you were challenged in this way?

Scenic Route

Let's focus on Jesus' response to the chief priests and elders after they agreed that the first son was the one who did what his father had asked. Jesus berated them while simultaneously giving honor to the people with whom he associated, namely people others had called sinners. The chief priests and elders were surely embarrassed by this conversation. They must have been mortified when Jesus said that the people whom they had been judging and condemning for so long would get into the kingdom of God before them. After all, they were the priests, the elders—the leaders of the people! Of course they wanted to go back and make Jesus answer their first question: By what authority are you saying these things? By all rights, these people were the ones who had authority, especially in the Temple.

I imagine there must have been a relatively large group of Jesus' supporters there at the time. Usually people who have power do not take well to having someone question their power, especially the priests in the midst of their own domain. It is hard to imagine that they would have allowed Jesus to speak to them that way if a large group of people hadn't been in opposition to them. They wanted to keep peace so that Rome would stay out of their affairs.

Jesus' answer has ramifications for our concept of the kingdom of God. Jesus said that the sinners, tax collectors, and prostitutes would enter the kingdom of God before the chief priests and the elders. Jesus appears to be saying that the chief priests and the elders would also enter the kingdom of God; they would just be behind the tax collectors and prostitutes and other "sinners."

One way of understanding Jesus' answer is that even those who failed to recognize Jesus and understand his revelation of the kingdom of God on earth will enter into that kingdom—but after those often viewed as less worthy. Of course, the chief priests and elders were among those who did not recognize Jesus' messiahship. As members of God's chosen people and ones who followed the Law to the fullest extent, the chief priests and elders would have expected to be a part of the kingdom of God. Certainly, they were offended that others might get there before them or be more worthy of entering.

The *Cumberland Presbyterian Confession of Faith* says "The covenant community is responsible to give witness to the mighty acts of God in the life, death, and resurrection of Jesus Christ. Where and when this witness is lacking, God is not without a witness. Therefore, it does not belong to the covenant community to judge where and in what manner God acts savingly through Jesus Christ" (5.31).

How might the composition of the listeners have affected the conversation between Jesus and the leaders of the Temple?

What do you think about the idea that even the chief priests and elders, the leaders of the Temple against whom Jesus was railing, entered the kingdom of God? How does this idea challenge your beliefs? How does it change the way you think about the kingdom of God?

What does the statement from our *Confession of Faith* mean to you?

When have you had a particularly frustrating encounter, perhaps on social media, where someone was trying to shame you or someone you know? How did you feel? What did you do to help? How did your actions change or perpetuate the status quo?

Upon whom do the people of your community look down? Why? What can you do to lift up those people?

Workers Ahead

Many of you are probably active on social media such as Facebook. I have an account, but I rarely post much on it, partially because it seems to have become a space for the honor/shame culture of our time. How often do people post something and only to have a of tug of war develop between people who oppose the view and people who agree with it? It is similar to the idea of trying to gain honor and perhaps even dispense a little shame about those things over which people disagree.

While Jesus used a similar kind of cultural approach to shame the chief priests and the elders, he was careful to avoid shaming those whom society already condemned. Jesus offered healing and forgiveness to sinners, tax collectors, adulterers, prostitutes, those with diseases, and others. He worked to build up in love those whom society had already beaten down. Those who thought themselves to be more important or more worthy of God's love were the ones Jesus worked to humble.

There is a lesson in this teaching for our day. We all live in somewhat different cultures according to our location, but there are always people whom society has shamed. This shaming comes specifically from people who feel they have more moral authority than others. Sometimes the church has gone along with these judgments. To follow in Jesus' footsteps, however, we need to be careful to give honor to those on whom society would stomp and ignore. We also need to help equalize things so that those who look down on others can learn that they are no better than anyone else. Where do we start? The answer is to look first inside ourselves. We may need to be ashamed for how we have treated others.

As we encounter people in our world, let us work to lift up those who are in need—physically, spiritually, emotionally, mentally, and in any other way—while we work to help others see these same people as humans worthy of their love.

In the Rear View

A lot happened in this short account of Jesus' run-in with the chief priests and elders. After his triumphal entry into the city the day before, and knowing what the next week held, Jesus was prepared when the religious authorities challenged him. His time was almost gone and he had to make the best possible use of what was left. By turning the question about authority back on the priests and elders, Jesus was able to continue to teach the crowds and put the religious leaders in their rightful place.

He showed them that the people on whom they had looked down as being sinners were the ones who were actually doing God's work. The priests and elders who had, with all sincerity, said "yes" to God were ignoring God's work.

Despite having taken on the religious authorities, Jesus stayed safe that day, probably because many of his supporters and friends were in the crowd. But his words had incensed the priests and elders. They would not back down easily.

> In what ways are you like the first son? the second son? What changes do you need to make in your life?

Travel Log

Day 1:

What makes you feel honor or shame? How does life sometimes become a contest for honor or shame? As you consider these questions, write down your responses. Try to add the root of those feelings. How can you exit the honor/shame system in your own life?

Day 2:

We often think of Jesus as a kind and peaceful man, but when we see stories like this one, we realize that Jesus was not afraid of conflict. Write down some things about which conflict, especially nonviolent conflict, may be justified. What is important enough for you to stand your ground? When have you done so? What was the result?

Day 3:

The priests and elders challenged Jesus' authority. What kind of authority did Jesus have? Write down ways that you can partner with Jesus and his authority to create change in your world.

Day 4:

Think of an example in your own life when you have been like the first son who said no but then went to work. Why did you initially say you wouldn't do whatever it was? What changed your mind? Journal a response to yourself about that moment.

Day 5:

Think of an example in your life when you were like the second son who quickly said yes but then ignored the work. Write down a brief description of that time and what caused you to act the way you did. How might you handle that situation differently now? What has caused you to change?

Day 6:

All of us have seen instances of injustice. The priests and elders were likely already trying to think of ways that they could shut Jesus up before this encounter was even over. Recall a time when you have seen an ugly exercise of power. How did it make you feel? What did you do or what can you do to change that for the future? Write down what occurred, as well as your ideas for change.

Day 7:

Jesus spent time with people whom others had already decided were not worth their time or love. Jesus turned those notions upside down by spending his time with the unwanted and unloved. Think of people in your circle of influence who may feel that they are unwanted or unloved. Think of people who have been ignored or debased by society. Write a plan of how you can bring light into the life of at least one of these people.

Wicked Tenants

Scripture for lesson: Matthew 21:33-44

As of the writing of this lesson, two Jewish cemeteries have recently been vandalized in the United States. One was in St. Louis, and the other in Philadelphia. For too long some people have hated others because of their religion. People have done evil things to one another in the name of God as well as out of greed. This parable includes both of these kinds of evil.

We must be especially careful when reading this parable, because it sometimes has been used by Christians to justify hatred and violence toward Jews. Hatred is surely not what God intended, nor is it likely the message Matthew wanted people to hear. With those words of caution, let us begin.

Prep for the Journey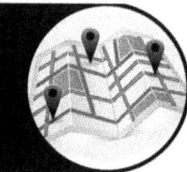

This parable is a continuation of the story from the previous lesson in this series. On Monday, after having entered Jerusalem the previous day to shouts of praise, Jesus returned to teach in the Temple. As he was teaching, some of the Temple leaders confronted him, questioning the authority by which he taught. Was it human authority or was it of God? Similar to the last passage, Jesus set up the Temple leaders by telling them a story and posing a leading question, which basically caused them to convict themselves.

Why do you think some Christians perpetrate hatred and violence toward people of other faiths?

Why do you think the Temple leaders continued to challenge Jesus?

When have you witnessed the undoing of someone who was confronted as being a hypocrite? What happened? What was that experience like?

On the Road

By the time Jesus told this parable, other people had joined the gathered crowd. Matthew added Pharisees to the list of religious leaders. Maybe someone sent for the Pharisees so that the priests and elders would have reinforcements. They were also experts in the Law, so their knowledge might have been needed to counter Jesus' teachings.

Jesus followed up the first parable with a second one. This one tells the story of a man who owned a vineyard.

Read Matthew 21:33-41.

"Listen to another parable. There was a landowner who planted a vineyard, put a fence around it, dug a wine press in it, and built a watchtower. Then he leased it to tenants and went to another country. ³ ⁴ When the harvest time had come, he sent his slaves to the tenants to collect his produce. ³⁵ But the tenants seized his slaves and beat one, killed another, and stoned another. ³⁶ Again he sent other slaves, more than the first; and they treated them in the same way. ³⁷ Finally he sent his son to them, saying, 'They will respect my son.' ³⁸ But when the tenants saw the son, they said to themselves, 'This is the heir; come, let us kill him and get his inheritance.' ³⁹ So they seized him, threw him out of the vineyard, and killed him. ⁴⁰ Now when the owner of the vineyard comes, what will he do to those tenants?" ⁴¹ They said to him, "He will put those wretches to a miserable death, and lease the vineyard to other tenants who will give him the produce at the harvest time."

It was common for people in New Testament times to lease land from someone. The tenants might have lived on the land to see that it was protected because, as in this case, the landowner was absent. After the harvest, they would have been responsible for paying either a portion of the crop or a percentage of the income to the landowner.

This landowner had seemingly done everything that was necessary for the vineyard to be successful. He planted it, fenced it, dug the wine press, and even built a watchtower. All of these things would have been common for this type of arrangement. While the grapes grew, the landowner went away.

In this parable, God becomes identified as the landowner and the tenants as the leaders of the Jewish people. Before we get into the behavior of the tenants, let's look at the landowner. Where did this landowner go? Was Jesus suggesting that God had gone away from the people or was absent in some way in the past?

Such questions are one of the challenges of interpreting parables. Sometimes the allegory seems pretty straightforward (in this case, that the landowner is God), but in other ways it becomes difficult. Jesus was not suggesting that God had ever left the people, but he told a story in a way that people could understand the point.

Who would be equivalent to the Pharisees and other religious leaders today? To whom might they turn for reinforcements?

When a landowner leases property today, what are his or her responsibilities? What are the responsibilities of the lessee?

What do you make of the landowner "going away?" How does that fit with the landowner representing God?

> Who are the tenants in the parable? How does your understanding of the tenants' identity affect the way you understand the parable?

The landowner sent slaves to the vineyard to collect his share of the crop. The tenants had known that this time would come, but rather than pay what was due, they chose to respond violently—killing the messengers.

The first set of slaves the landowner sent probably represented the early prophets of the Old Testament. God sent them as messengers to the people, but the people did not want to hear what they had to say. Often the prophets were ill-treated.

Given that the messengers were killed, we don't know how the landowner learned what had happened. Perhaps he didn't know, but when the first group failed to return, he simply sent the second group. Those slaves would have represented the later prophets in the Old Testament. They were also beaten, stoned, and killed.

Then the landowner decided to send his own son, who should have been viewed as if he were the landowner. But the tenants saw a possibility. The laws of Jesus' time were different than today. Possession of the land was the biggest part of becoming an owner. So, if the owner was away and the only other person to have a claim to that land was dead, the tenants would reasonably have concluded that the land would then be theirs. Obviously, Jesus was the son sent by God, the landowner.

> How would you respond to Jesus' question? Why? In what ways might you also be convicting yourself?

All this time, the chief priests, elders, and Pharisees had apparently not caught on to what Jesus was saying. When he concluded the story and asked what the landowner should do, they responded as many people might have: Go to the vineyard and kill those wicked tenants. Then secure new tenants who were honest and faithful. And thus, they convicted themselves.

Scenic Route

Read Matthew 21:42-44.
Jesus said to them, "Have you never read in the scriptures:

'The stone that the builders rejected
  has become the cornerstone;
this was the Lord's doing,
  and it is amazing in our eyes'?

[43] Therefore I tell you, the kingdom of God will be taken away from you and given to a people that produces the fruits of the kingdom. [44] The one who falls on this stone will be broken to pieces; and it will crush anyone on whom it falls."

Jesus brought down the hammer on the Temple leaders. They had been drawn in by his story, and by the time it became evident that Jesus had been talking about them, they had agreed with his point. That is, they agreed with the point he was making about the landowner and the tenants. The story clearly shows that the tenants had acted with malicious intent, resorting to murder to achieve their own financial gain. Anyone could see the evil of their actions. But when Jesus applied this story to the leaders of the Jewish faith, and especially when he applied the role of the son to himself, the Temple leaders were extremely offended.

There seems to have been a lot of support for Jesus from the people who were at the Temple. Remember that many of Jesus' followers were the poor and downtrodden. His teachings offered them hope. The leaders of the Temple didn't want such people to be considered as their equals. They took advantage of this group's lack of education and/or skills to keep them in poverty. Since the religious leaders were the ones who interpreted the Law and created new laws as they felt necessary, they probably kept their own best interests at heart more often than not. If the masses of poor people had revolted by following Jesus, the entire nation would have been in upheaval.

It's no wonder that the religious leaders wanted to get rid of Jesus. They wanted to arrest him immediately before he gained any more popularity. Yet they could not, because a great number of the people in the crowd agreed with Jesus. Arresting Jesus would have been political suicide.

Remember that Jesus and the people around him were Jewish, just as were the Temple leaders. But Jesus struck a chord with the people by speaking about the way the leaders of the Temple had not fulfilled their duty. Throughout the history of the Israelites, prophets had been sent to tell the Temple leaders and the kings that they must change. But the messages of the prophets were largely ignored.

Finally, Jesus said, God sent the Son because the people would receive and believe the Son. Many of the people did believe him and believe in him, but most of the leaders did not. They wanted to get rid of him because he insulted them and threatened their positions.

Of course Jesus was right, but it must have been difficult for the leaders to hear what he said, much less even begin to accept his words. These leaders were career servants of the Temple system. They likely hadn't done much to change that system; they simply kept the same processes as their predecessors. They would have argued that it was not the ways in which they managed the Temple and kept the rituals that should have been questioned, but rather Jesus' accusations. It is likely that many would have agreed with them. To them, Jesus was an unimportant teacher from outside Jerusalem. They hadn't felt a need to take him seriously until people started listening to him.

But that was Jesus' point. For too long the Temple leaders had simply maintained the status quo, failing to realize how their system was oppressing their own people, ignoring the most vulnerable in the

---

As a follower of Jesus, how might you have felt listening to this exchange between the leaders of the Temple and Jesus?

To what groups of people do today's leaders feel superior? How do their feelings affect actions and laws that impact those people over whom they have expressed superiority?

What prophetic messages are we failing to hear today? Why?

How might you have felt if you were a leader of the Temple and found yourself caught in the web that Jesus had created? How might you have tried to defend yourself?

How effectively does the United States maintain a separation of church and state? In what ways is such a separation beneficial/harmful to those who are vulnerable?

How can Christians today resist the violent tendencies that some have against neighbors, enemies, and nations? What do you think Jesus would make of these tendencies?

What messages do Christians send to others when we fight amongst ourselves?

What modern teachings are at odds with Jesus' teaching? How can the church equip people to resist teachings that contradict Jesus' example, whether outside or inside the church?

society, and not following the words of the prophets. The leaders had benefited from this system, but many people, including those who followed Jesus, had been left out of the good times, especially as the leaders became more entangled with the Roman government.

Workers Ahead

At the beginning of this lesson, I mentioned that this parable has been used in the past to justify dislike or even violence toward the Jewish people. But it is important to note that Jesus would not, as a Jew, have condemned the entire Jewish people. It seems more likely that Jesus was condemning a certain group and/or perhaps a certain way of following the Jewish faith.

Remember that many of the controversies in the early church were not between Christians and Jews, but between different groups of Jews. With that being the case, we can easily relate. There are often conflicts between different groups of Christians. We hope that these conflicts will not spill over into conflict between Christians and people of other world religions.

In the Sermon on the Mount, Jesus taught that people should love their enemies. This doesn't seem like the kind of person who would endorse violence against those who didn't agree with him. In fact, the Temple leaders are the ones who responded that the wicked tenants should be put to death.

For people today, this parable is a constant reminder that to be faithful followers of Jesus, we have to look back continually to what Jesus did and what Jesus stood for, comparing our words and actions to his ideals. I am afraid that many modern Christians, if they took that task seriously, would find that the things over which they argue are either not important to Jesus or are in actual opposition to Jesus' teaching.

In the Rear View

This parable is difficult to hear. The violent tone of the tenants was matched by the way the leaders of the Temple expected the landowner to respond to those tenants. We have to read these words wondering if this is the way a merciful God will react to the faithless. And if so, how will any of us fare?

I hope this parable can help us to set aside our violent tendencies and instead take time to examine our lives within the framework of what Jesus taught. Jesus embodied faithfulness and accepted all who came to him who were repentant.

How should we live so that Jesus will accept us?

What attitudes do you need to set aside so that your life will reflect Jesus' teachings?

Travel Log

Day 1:

List things for which you are grateful. Remember that God owns all, and we are caretakers of these things only for a little while. How can we best bring honor to God by caring for the things we have received?

Day 2:

Imagine yourself as a leader of the Temple in Jesus' day. When Jesus uses his parables to accuse you of being a faithless tenant, how do you respond? Journal your reflections.

Day 3:

People in the Temple area were apparently drawn to this conversation. If you were one of those people, not knowing anything about Jesus, how might you react to his words? What would you tell your family about what happened at the Temple that day? Make some notes about your thoughts.

Day 4:

How do you view this parable differently knowing that Jesus was continuing to bring the same message that God had given to the prophets? Who are the prophets of today? What message are they bringing? How are they received by the Church? Jot down some things you think prophets are telling us today or some things they should be telling us.

Day 5:
   Think of a time when someone has challenged your beliefs or actions. Perhaps this was in a time when you were in a position of authority. How did you feel? Write down some things that happened in that challenge that were not fair or correct, but also try to think of things that you might have learned from that experience. How can you be prepared to learn when others challenge you?

Day 6:
   Take a few moments to write on the similarities and differences between the challenges that Jesus represented to the Temple structure and challenges the Church faces today. How can we adopt Jesus' demeanor to help make the Church a greater vessel for God?

Day 7:

Contact a friend or confidant to talk about your thoughts regarding this parable. Talk to your friend about some of the questions raised in this lesson. Write down a few things that you want to remember from that conversation in the space below.

Save the Date!

Scripture for lesson: Matthew 22:1-14

> What are some memories you have about weddings?
>
> What occasions, such as a royal wedding, do people really want to attend? Why would they particularly want to attend? What might cause all the invitees to decline at the last moment?

Weddings are beautiful and important occasions. There are few other times in the church when as many people come together in one place, and basically all those people are happy. Usually weddings are a great opportunity to catch up with family, to share gifts and good wishes for two people who are just beginning a life together, and to witness the gift of love in one of the most intimate relationships possible between humans. Speaking as a pastor, I can say that weddings are some of my most joyous times in ministry.

The parable examined in this lesson is about a wedding, but not just any wedding. The king's son was getting married. You can imagine how wonderful it would be to celebrate with the royal family at such a happy, momentous time.

Just think back to the royal weddings that have occurred during the past twenty or so years. In that span of time, there have been royal weddings in Norway, Denmark, Tonga, Indonesia, Monaco, India, Jordan, England, and many other countries. Many of us are more likely familiar with the royal weddings in England due to the relationship between our countries and the media coverage. Who wouldn't want to go to an event such as the wedding of William and Kate or Charles and Diana? Who would turn down that invitation? Just imagine how many people would be lined up to take that invitation if you had to opt out?

Prep for the Journey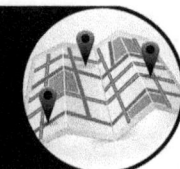

If you have been studying the lessons in this volume in order, you will likely recognize that this parable directly follows the previous parables of the two sons and the wicked tenants. Many times Jesus' parables came in threes, increasing in importance and urgency. The third, then, is often the most forceful statement of the point Jesus was making, with each parable having roughly the same message.

The other two parables were about the faithful people of God and those who would be discovered as being unfaithful. Just prior to the first parable about the two sons, Matthew said that Jesus cursed a fig tree because it was not producing fruit. The fig tree withered and died. This incident gives us a clue about the underlying goal of these three parables.

Fig trees produce their fruit in warmer climates starting around June. The cursing of the fig tree in the Gospel happened at the beginning of the week before Passover, much too early for the tree to have been producing fruit. The action was symbolic: The fig tree was a symbol of the existing Temple system. The leaders and the system itself were not bearing fruit. Matthew included this story at the beginning of this set of three parables because he wanted to make a point about the current system. Because it was not bearing fruit, it would be replaced.

Then Matthew tells these three stories about people who were expected to be faithful but who turned out to be unfaithful. In each case, they were replaced by someone else or a different group. Perhaps the most shocking example is found in the scripture for this lesson.

> When have you expected to find fruit in a relationship or in a work environment only to find nothing? How did you react?

> What happens when the time comes to replace the fig tree because it isn't producing fruit?

> Why systems or people today are not bearing fruit and need to be replaced?

On the Road

Most people have accepted an invitation with the intent of going only to change their minds closer to the time of the event. Maybe something happens that prevents them from attending. Some people will also accept an invitation and then forget about going until it is too late. Others will accept because they don't want to offend the host, but have no intention of going. Each of these situations is probably represented by the people in this parable.

Read Matthew 22:1-10.

Once more Jesus spoke to them in parables, saying: ² "The kingdom of heaven may be compared to a king who gave a wedding banquet for his son. ³ He sent his slaves to call those who had been invited to the wedding banquet, but they would not come. ⁴ Again he sent other slaves, saying, 'Tell those who have been invited: Look, I have prepared my dinner, my oxen and my fat calves have been slaughtered, and everything is ready; come to the wedding banquet.' ⁵ But they made light of it and went away, one to his farm, another to his business, ⁶ while the rest seized his slaves, mistreated them, and killed them. ⁷ The king was enraged. He sent his troops, destroyed those murderers, and burned their city. ⁸ Then he said to his slaves, 'The wedding is ready, but those

> When have you not been able to fulfill an obligation to attend an event? Why? When has someone failed to attend something that you were hosting? How did you feel? respond?

invited were not worthy. ⁹ Go therefore into the main streets, and invite everyone you find to the wedding banquet.' ¹⁰ Those slaves went out into the streets and gathered all whom they found, both good and bad; so the wedding hall was filled with guests.

The first part of the story presents the unusual circumstance of people being unwilling to go to an elaborate feast in honor of the king's son's wedding. This same story is in the Gospel of Luke as well as in the non-canonical Gospel of Thomas. In those settings, some of the details are different. The people who were invited give excuses as to why they cannot come, and the violent acts of the invitees and the king are not present. But the inclusion of this story in so many different settings suggests that the message was an important part of the newly formed (and continually forming) Christian community.

While the message is relatively clear in each setting, Matthew's version is particularly explicit and frightening. As we have seen in other parables, the king seems to represent God, and the son represents Jesus, the Christ. The wedding banquet is prepared for those who would have a relationship with God. People had been notified about the banquet and invited to participate in it well in advance.

In Jesus' world, it was common to set a general date for a wedding, but not as specifically as we would set one for a modern celebration. Sometimes things took extra time, so it was a common practice for the servants of the king to be prepared to notify the guests when the feast was ready.

Where things went wrong, however, was when the servants notified people that the time had come for the wedding to occur. While Luke and Thomas give reasons that the people didn't come, Matthew says they "made light" of the invitation. Denying the invitation of a king was a big deal, and a large crowd of people doing this at the same time would have been like a revolt of the people.

Matthew offers a longer version of the story of invitation into fellowship with God. The first set of slaves whom the king sent to gather the invitees represents the prophets from the Old Testament. The people simply ignored them. The second set probably indicates the first followers of Jesus who offered the invitation from God to the people. At first they were treated with scorn, but as they continued to offer the invitation, they were killed. Matthew explained that those who do the work of God will sometimes be hurt or even martyred, but as servants of the king (God), they must do what they were asked to do.

When the king found out about these killings, he was incensed. Of course, it is impossible to think of this story as one we are supposed to understand literally. The king did not keep dinner on the warmers while he raised an army, killed all the people, and burned down their city. The city was apparently his own city, anyway. But the threat is there that God will destroy those who resist God and replace them with others who may have never received an invitation, but who are then welcomed into God's banquet for the son.

How do you feel about the king representing God in this parable? Why?

Why might the people have declined an invitation from the king? To what type of event would you compare this situation today?

What do you think of the violence in this parable? In what way is it surprising? Why might the people of that time have found it necessary?

This is just what happens. Another round of slaves was sent into the streets to fill up the banquet hall. All were welcomed without restriction. They were there because the king was having a banquet and he wanted to share it, not because they were worthy of it.

This might create a logical problem. The people who were first invited were considered "unworthy" of being included, but the second group of people were not judged to be worthy or unworthy. They were just invited, regardless of their worth.

> What do you think about the idea of worthiness expressed in this parable?

Scenic Route

Read Matthew 22:11-14.

"But when the king came in to see the guests, he noticed a man there who was not wearing a wedding robe, ¹² and he said to him, 'Friend, how did you get in here without a wedding robe?' And he was speechless. ¹³ Then the king said to the attendants, 'Bind him hand and foot, and throw him into the outer darkness, where there will be weeping and gnashing of teeth.' ¹⁴ For many are called, but few are chosen."

This second part of the story may leave us scratching our heads. Some of the information in it, which is only presented in Matthew's Gospel, is confusing. In terms of the purpose of this section, it can even be distracting.

At the conclusion of the earlier passage, the king sent his slaves out into the world to bring anybody and everybody into the wedding banquet. Those who were originally invited were found to be unworthy, but everyone else, good or bad, was invited.

If we take this to mean that, since the feast was already prepared, these people were just brought in off the streets, we have to wonder how in the world someone was supposed to know to have a wedding robe on hand. Maybe we should ask why there were so many people at the banquet who had the right kind of attire, rather than why one person wasn't dressed properly.

> What do you think about anybody and everybody being invited to the banquet? What does that say for the church of today? How well is the church living out that invitation?

If we look at this from a worldly point of view, we might imagine that kings can be pretty sensitive people. Any real or imagined slight might cause them to become angry. The clothing worn to a wedding was intended to honor the wedding party. It would have been even more important to wear the right kind of clothing when attending a royal wedding. So, the idea that one would be in the wrong type of clothing could be considered offensive to the king who was hosting the party. But we come back to the question of why these people from off the street would be expected to be wearing clothing that was appropriate for a wedding banquet. Some of them probably didn't even have access to such clothing.

> How can the availability of proper clothing become an obstacle to participating in the church?

Like the violent acts that were in the previous part of the story, we have to think of these events as teaching a lesson. In the early church, and in some cases now, when someone sets aside their earlier way of life and becomes a follower of Christ, they are said to have "put on new clothing." Their old ways of being and getting along in the world no longer fit them. They have changed themselves and a symbol of that is changing their clothing.

Those who were invited into the banquet may not have been judged as worthy or unworthy when they entered, but upon entering, they were expected to change. They figuratively changed their clothing and became followers of Christ. Although there seemed to be no cost or no barrier to their entry, there was a price. They had to become followers who were willing to celebrate with the king and his son.

This one man who did not have on the right attire seems to have been unwilling to change who he was so that he could fit in with the banquet. Even seeing the lavishness, the wonder, the beauty of the celebration, he apparently tried to remain the same as he was before and still enjoy the banquet. That, said Jesus, simply isn't possible.

Workers Ahead

Jesus prefaced this parable by saying that this is what the kingdom of heaven is like. When we have our eyes set on the kingdom, we can understand this parable and see how it should affect our lives. We can see what trying to delay acceptance of God is like, what setting aside the invitation to be part of God's party is like. We can also understand that we only have the opportunity to be a part of that banquet because of grace, not because of how good or bad we are.

There are churches where people have been made to feel less than welcome because they did not have the proper clothing. Maybe their skin was a different color or maybe they had tattoos. They weren't like those who were already there. While we must change our actions and attitude to be welcomed at the banquet, we also need to be careful that we do not exclude those whom God has invited.

What parts of yourself have you been unwilling to change? Why?

How have you changed your attire to be fit for the wedding banquet?

What might cause someone to set aside God's invitation to the banquet?

What gets in your way of changing? How do you feel about people who are unlike you also being welcomed at the banquet?

In the Rear View

This parable has some disturbing sections of violence, and it was intended to be the most shocking of the three parables in a row, which started with Matthew 21:18. We have looked at the possible implications of being a person who was invited to the banquet but didn't take the invitation seriously. We have seen what happened to those who harmed the king's servants who were sent to gather the wedding guests. And we have even seen what happens when people are allowed in, but are unwilling to change for the party.

We are then left with these questions: Who are we in this parable? How will we work to become people who are allowed to stay at God's party?

Travel Log

Day 1:

Jesus told this parable in the presence of his disciples and the Pharisees. Write down what you might have experienced in that place. What might you have felt? How might you have responded? What emotions were others displaying?

Day 2:

Put yourself in the position of a bystander in the crowd. You've heard of Jesus, but don't know anything about his teachings. On the other hand, you have been taught to follow the Law, which the religious leaders make a point of doing. Jesus is criticizing these very leaders that you have been taught to respect and follow. How do you feel as Jesus criticizes the leaders? How do you interpret Jesus' parables? How do you feel about the leaders after listening to Jesus teach? Journal your responses to these questions.

Day 3:

Imagine yourself as one of the religious leaders who was present when Jesus told these parables, which seem to be pointing at you. How do you react? What influence does the crowd have on your reaction? Why?

Consider the religious leaders in your life. How might they react to this parable? Write a prayer for those who lead your church and denomination.

Day 4:

Think of a time when you were invited to be a part of something that might have been wonderful, but you decided to ignore the invitation. What caused you to choose not to participate? How did you feel when you heard about the event from others? What parallels do you see between that situation and this parable? Jot down some of your thoughts.

Day 5:
   Jesus said that when the king asked the man who was dressed improperly how he had gotten into the celebration, the man was speechless. Write a speech for him. Maybe it is a rationalization, maybe it is a confession. What might you expect or want him to say?

Day 6:
   The violence in the middle part of this parable could be disturbing. How do you feel about the invitees' responses to the servants? the king's actions? How are they necessary to the meaning of the parable? How do the violent actions increase the urgency of listening to the parable?
   Unfortunately, violence has become so common in our society that it does not seem to create the urgency it once did. However, we must do something to decrease the violence that surrounds us. Write a letter to the leaders of your community, state, and our nation, stating your concerns and asking for their help in making changes.

Day 7:
    Take a moment to think of yourself as you were or are becoming a Christian. When we enter into the banquet, we must be willing to change ourselves. What are you unwilling to let go of as you enter the banquet? List those things and explore why you are unwilling to release them.

Out of Oil!

Scripture for lesson: Matthew 25:1-13

I often talk with my kids about what life was like in the old days—you know, back in the 1980s. We have a subscription to a television streaming service, and my kids can watch every episode of a television show back to back to back. Before you worry about them too much, their mother and I don't let them watch that much television, but it is always there, ready to be viewed.

We try to explain that not too long ago you actually had to wait a week to see the next episode of the show you were watching. If you missed it, you'd better hope that you had set the VCR, because there was no "on demand," or other service that could help you catch up.

These reflections caused me to think about waiting. As a society, we try to avoid waiting; many people simply don't deal well with any type of delays. We've gone from writing letters to making phone calls to sending emails to texting. We've gone from walking to riding horses to driving cars to flying on airplanes. We've gone from no Internet to the dial-up modem to high-speed Internet. There are now so many things we can get instantly.

Waiting is hard. Being prepared to wait can be even harder, as this parable teaches.

> **When have you had to wait for something about which you were excited? How did you react if it was delayed?**

Prep for the Journey

The parable we are studying today is a little awkward for us, partially because we don't have much information about the wedding practices of people in Jesus' time. But even if we had more information, it is likely that it wouldn't line up with the details given in this passage. Even in Matthew's other writings about wedding celebrations, there is nothing that seems like this parable. In Matthew 24 we have the story of the wedding banquet in which everyone was invited to the groom's home. In chapter 9, verse 15, Matthew also spoke of

> **What are some wedding customs today? What changes have you noticed in wedding customs?**

the presence of a bridegroom, but there was no mention of bridesmaids.

Add to this that scholars consider the Greek word translated in the NRSV as "bridesmaids" is probably better translated as "virgins," and we have an unusual circumstance. Ten virgins were waiting for the arrival of a bridegroom, there was no mention of the bride, and they were going to be taken in with him for an unknown purpose. Those who weren't there at the time he arrived would not be allowed in later.

This situation was used to make a point, but the likelihood that an actual wedding celebration would have been like this one is pretty low. However, if we have our eyes and ears open to the symbols Matthew uses, we will see and hear Jesus' message for his early followers, and perhaps especially for Matthew's community of believers.

> How do you feel about this parable being a contrived situation used to make a point? How might those who heard it originally have reacted since it apparently did not reflect actual traditions?

On the Road

Read Matthew 25:1-13.

"Then the kingdom of heaven will be like this. Ten bridesmaids took their lamps and went to meet the bridegroom. ² Five of them were foolish, and five were wise. ³ When the foolish took their lamps, they took no oil with them; ⁴ but the wise took flasks of oil with their lamps. ⁵ As the bridegroom was delayed, all of them became drowsy and slept. ⁶ But at midnight there was a shout, 'Look! Here is the bridegroom! Come out to meet him.' ⁷ Then all those bridesmaids got up and trimmed their lamps. ⁸ The foolish said to the wise, 'Give us some of your oil, for our lamps are going out.' ⁹ But the wise replied, 'No! there will not be enough for you and for us; you had better go to the dealers and buy some for yourselves.' ¹⁰ And while they went to buy it, the bridegroom came, and those who were ready went with him into the wedding banquet; and the door was shut. ¹¹ Later the other bridesmaids came also, saying, 'Lord, lord, open to us.' ¹² But he replied, 'Truly I tell you, I do not know you.' ¹³ Keep awake therefore, for you know neither the day nor the hour."

Jesus began the story with a common phrase: "Then the kingdom of heaven will be like this." It was a signal that he would explain some mystery about the kingdom of heaven in a story or a short saying. These stories or sayings usually only addressed one aspect of the kingdom, but many of them are difficult for us to understand. Generally we should not try to analyze them too deeply as if every small detail has to fit into the understanding, but instead we should try to catch the broad message of what Jesus was saying. This story is no different.

Jesus compared the kingdom of heaven to a wedding banquet. Typically when marriage language is used in the Bible, God is seen

> In what other instances do you remember Jesus using the phrase, *The kingdom of God is like...*? How are those similar to this usage? How are they different?

> How do you prepare for the unknown? How confident do you feel that you are ready to face whatever comes?
>
> When have you been part of a group in which some people made wise decisions and others foolish ones? How did you influence those decisions?
>
> How do you handle waiting? How does the reason for the wait affect your response? How is your response affected by what you are waiting for?
>
> When have you missed out on an opportunity because you weren't prepared? How did you feel about the experience?
>
> What helps you to live a godly life even though the reward is not in sight? How do you feel about considering entrance to God's kingdom as a reward?

as the groom and the people of Israel are the bride. In the New Testament Jesus is the groom and the Church is the bride. But Jesus altered the image for the purposes of this story. Jesus wanted to make the point that some of those who were waiting for the kingdom were not doing the things they needed to do. On the other hand, some people were preparing well.

The Church is represented by the ten bridesmaids, or virgins. They all seemed to be equally anxious for the arrival of the bridegroom, but the text tells us that five were foolish and five were wise. It would have been impossible to tell the difference in the bridesmaids without an explanation. The explanation provides knowledge needed later in the parable.

Some of the bridesmaids brought extra oil, but others didn't. We gather that none of them were expecting to wait long for the bridegroom to arrive. The bridegroom in this parable is Jesus himself, at his second coming, and the Church, represented by the bridesmaids, is encouraged to be prepared, even if the bridegroom is delayed.

The bridesmaids were prepared and eagerly waited to receive the bridegroom. They expected him at any moment. They waited. And they waited. And they waited some more. Finally, they all grew tired and fell asleep.

It is important to note that, even though the last verse in the parable exhorts the people to stay awake, it wasn't because some fell asleep that they were not allowed into the banquet. All of the bridesmaids fell asleep. It was the ones who were prepared for a wait that was longer than expected who were allowed into the banquet.

When the bridegroom finally came, the foolish bridesmaids had run out of oil. The others had extra, but they were unwilling to share it, so the foolish bridesmaids went out to buy more. This was not the time of 24-hour stores, nor, I imagine, of 24-hour oil dealers. The idea that these women could go out at midnight and buy oil and come back is pretty far-fetched. Still, having no other choice, the women did as they were told, and left. While they were gone, the bridegroom came and took the wise bridesmaids into the banquet with him.

In Jewish literature, oil is a symbol of good deeds. The care of others and the keeping of the commandment to love God and to love others seem to be caught up in the opportunity to enter into the kingdom of heaven. If oil represents godly living, then it becomes clear why the wise bridesmaids did not share their oil with the others. The foolish bridesmaids cannot borrow or take godly living from anyone. They must work toward that themselves.

It is one thing to accept the word of God and be loving and merciful for a short period of time, but to do so day after day, month after month, year after year as you wait for the reward, the coming of the bridegroom, is much harder. Assuming that the oil does represent godly living, it seems that the foolish bridesmaids tired of that kind of living, and failed to sustain it. But even though the wise bridesmaids did tire, they had enough reserves so that they were still prepared.

Scenic Route

Each Gospel presents the story of Jesus with a different objective. The Gospels themselves were written years after Jesus' death and resurrection. The Gospel of Matthew was written between 75 and 100 C.E. Modern scholars think it is a rewriting of Mark's Gospel with an additional source that was also used by the author of the Gospel of Luke.

The differences in these three Gospels can be partially explained by the passage of time. Over that time, stories may have changed slightly, or other memories or stories about Jesus' life may have come to light. But just as important as how these differences came about is the information those particular writers were trying to reveal to the world.

Each Gospel was written with a particular audience in mind and it is widely believed that Matthew was writing primarily to a Jewish audience. The sometimes seemingly cruel tone that he took regarding some Jews was indicative of a conflict between different groups of Jews, not a conflict between Christians and the entire Jewish religion. Matthew was also trying to encourage believers who were frustrated by the Roman occupation and rule. These people were confused by the amount of time it was taking for Jesus to come back to redeem the earth and its people.

With that in mind, it is likely that Matthew altered or embellished the parable we are considering today. Some scholars think Matthew might have invented this parable as a way to encourage the believers who were so tired of waiting for Jesus to return. They had received the message of Christ, and they were willing to follow in Christ's footsteps, but they, like Christians in many other communities, had expected that Jesus' return would be a lot sooner. Some followers were probably growing weary, perhaps even beginning to question whether Jesus was going to return.

Matthew presented this story that was intended to encourage them to keep the faith. Keep on doing what Christ commanded. It addresses the fact that we all grow weary of waiting. Even the wise bridesmaids slept while they waited. But when the time came, they had done their homework, they had followed Christ's commands, and they were ready. When the bridegroom finally came to be with them, they were allowed into the banquet. When Jesus finally comes to be with the people, they will need to be ready.

What difference, if any, does knowing that the Gospel writers addressed specific audiences affect how we read and understand their writings?

What do you think it meant for Matthew's community to be prepared? What does it mean for you? for your faith community?

What encourages you to keep the faith when you become tired? How can you offer such encouragement to others?

Workers Ahead

We all want to be prepared for the coming of Christ, but we have been waiting for a very long time. Generation after generation has expected Jesus to come, and it has not happened yet. It is one thing to keep our lamps filled with oil and trimmed for a night, for weeks, or for a season. But it is hard to think of being constantly prepared for our whole lifetime, let alone for almost 2,000 years.

Perhaps instead of constantly looking forward to the coming of Christ, we would do our best to live each day working to emulate Christ. That seems to be what Matthew was suggesting the wise bridesmaids had done. They had continued their works of charity and love for God and for others even as they were preparing for the coming of the bridegroom.

We do not know when Christ will return, but if we spend all our time trying to calculate that time or looking for it to happen, we may miss opportunities to grow in Christ here and now. If we are constantly looking for Jesus to come and invite us into the banquet, we may fail to do the work God has for us or miss opportunities to share our faith with others. It is good to look forward to that time, but we must take care not to look past our own time, when the work of Christ still needs to be done in this world.

> How can we prepare for Christ's coming without becoming obsessed with it?
>
> What works is God calling you to do? What opportunities to share your faith may you have been failing to use?

In the Rear View

In this lesson, we have examined the parable of the ten bridesmaids. It seems likely that this story wasn't really about a wedding banquet, but was constructed to teach us about preparing for the coming of Jesus. We must remember to carry out Jesus' word in our daily lives even as we keep one eye toward the coming glory of Christ's return. As we do this, we will be preparing ourselves to be welcomed into that glorious wedding feast.

Travel Log

Day 1:
What does it mean for Christ to come again? What are you expecting at Christ's return? Reflect on these questions and write down some things for which you are hoping, and perhaps some things that concern you.

Day 2:
The oil of godly living was a theme in this lesson. What are some examples of that oil in your daily life? List three concrete ways that you can work toward living a more godly life. Make plans to implement these ideas.

Day 3:
Imagine what it must have been like to be one of the five bridesmaids who was invited into the banquet. What might the bridesmaids have seen? tasted? smelled? heard? felt? Journal your thoughts.

Day 4:
Think about the bridesmaids who were excluded from the banquet. Imagine their disappointment and distress when the bridegroom announced that he did not know them. Write about that moment as if you were one of those five women.

Day 5:

Matthew was writing to encourage a group of Christians who were growing weary of waiting. How often do you think about how Christians today are waiting for the coming of Christ? What emotions are stirred in you? Write a letter of encouragement to someone you know who is struggling in his or her faith.

Day 6:

How have you prepared for Christ's return? What obstacles have you encountered to those preparations? How difficult is it to keep yourself ready when the time is unknown? As you reflect on those questions, write down your thoughts.

Day 7:
The banquet will come one day. As the body of Christ, we hope that all will be invited into that banquet. Note some ways that we can help others to prepare for that great banquet. How can you encourage others to follow in Christ's footsteps?

Investments that Pay

Scripture for lesson: Matthew 25:14-30

Probably some of you, like me, are saving for retirement. And maybe some of you, like me, get nervous almost every time you put money into that account. When we put money away, especially when we invest, we have to know that while we want that money to gain value, it is possible that our investments may lose money. It is even possible that we will lose all that we have invested.

Safeguards are in place that are supposed to protect our investments, but as we found out a few years ago, even when we think we have done a good job of protecting what is ours, we may still lose substantial amounts of money. Several people had to delay their retirement after the most recent downturn in the markets.

Investing is always a risk, and for those in ancient Palestine, I can only assume that the risks were even greater. As we read this story about the three slaves who were given property belonging to their master, we have to keep in mind the real fear of losing that original investment. Otherwise, the actions of the slaves and the urgency of the need to do something with what we have been given seem less significant or, well, frightening.

> When have you been concerned about an investment—of time, money, or effort—and wondered whether that investment was going to pay off?
>
> How do you attempt to safeguard your investments of time and money?

Prep for the Journey

This parable is the final one in Jesus' stories about the coming of the Son of Man and the importance of being prepared for his return. We have been reading in Matthew about judgment and what that judgment will look like. Jesus silenced the leaders of the Temple, and then he sat down with his followers to teach them about the coming kingdom. But the message in these later teachings seems harsher. It is more about the coming judgment and the need to be prepared for the coming of the Messiah than it is words of comfort about the poor and the needy being welcomed into the kingdom.

> Why do you think the tone of Jesus' teachings changed from the earlier part of his ministry? Why might some of the change be attributable to Matthew?

In this passage, we find a new message about responsibility. What is the responsibility of those who would join the banquet or enter into the joy of their master? In the parable from the last lesson, Jesus compared those who wait faithfully to virgins who had had the forethought to bring extra oil to the vigil of awaiting the bridegroom's arrival. In this lesson, Jesus compared the faithful to the slaves who were entrusted with their master's money.

In the context of what Matthew wrote, we have to remember that the second coming had, for Matthew, already been delayed. Matthew did not foresee Christians like us reading these words almost two thousand years in the future. He was confused because Jesus hadn't already returned. He was so certain that Jesus would be returning soon that his writing reflects his feeling that surely there were some alive in his time who would see the second coming.

For Matthew, the time to get things together is the present. Tomorrow is not guaranteed. If we aren't faithful, or if we put off the things we ought to do, we will be caught unprepared. Matthew assured us that we do not want to be unprepared.

> **Why is it important always to be prepared? How difficult do you find it to remain prepared when Jesus' second coming continues to be delayed?**

On the Road

We all know that not every person is equally abled. Some people have the ability to program computers to do mind-boggling tasks; others can preach a sermon that will bring the haughtiest people to their knees; and others can reach out to someone who is lonely or hurting, offering time, comfort, and a listening ear. Each ability is important and needed, but you would obviously not ask all three persons to do the same thing and expect the same results.

Read Matthew 25:14-30.

"For it is as if a man, going on a journey, summoned his slaves and entrusted his property to them; ^{15} to one he gave five talents, to another two, to another one, to each according to his ability. Then he went away. ^{16} The one who had received the five talents went off at once and traded with them, and made five more talents. ^{17} In the same way, the one who had the two talents made two more talents. ^{18} But the one who had received the one talent went off and dug a hole in the ground and hid his master's money. ^{19} After a long time the master of those slaves came and settled accounts with them. ^{20} Then the one who had received the five talents came forward, bringing five more talents, saying, 'Master, you handed over to me five talents; see, I have made five more talents.' ^{21} His master said to him, 'Well done, good and trustworthy slave; you have been trustworthy in a few things, I will put you in charge of many

> **What are you able to do for God? How do you feel about your ability?**

things; enter into the joy of your master.' ²² And the one with the two talents also came forward, saying, 'Master, you handed over to me two talents; see, I have made two more talents.' ²³ His master said to him, 'Well done, good and trustworthy slave; you have been trustworthy in a few things, I will put you in charge of many things; enter into the joy of your master.' ²⁴ Then the one who had received the one talent also came forward, saying, 'Master, I knew that you were a harsh man, reaping where you did not sow, and gathering where you did not scatter seed; ²⁵ so I was afraid, and I went and hid your talent in the ground. Here you have what is yours.' ²⁶ But his master replied, 'You wicked and lazy slave! You knew, did you, that I reap where I did not sow, and gather where I did not scatter? ²⁷ Then you ought to have invested my money with the bankers, and on my return I would have received what was my own with interest. ²⁸ So take the talent from him, and give it to the one with the ten talents. ²⁹ For to all those who have, more will be given, and they will have an abundance; but from those who have nothing, even what they have will be taken away. ³⁰ As for this worthless slave, throw him into the outer darkness, where there will be weeping and gnashing of teeth.'"

As we have seen before, Jesus used this story as an allegory. This time, Jesus was the man, or as he is called later in the story, the master. The slaves were Jesus' disciples. Of course, Matthew envisions Jesus' disciples to be not only the original twelve, but all the followers of Jesus who were part of the Christian fellowship.

The money that the slaves were given to manage was a sum that few of the people listening could even have imagined having in their possession. Since one talent was worth 15 years of a laborer's salary, five talents were worth 75 years of a laborer's salary! It was an enormous sum to entrust to anyone.

The master left these large sums of money in the charge of three slaves, according to their ability. We do not have information at the beginning of the story as to why the master trusts one with five talents, and one with two talents and one with one talent, just that they were given these responsibilities according to their ability.

Quickly it became apparent that the master had good judgment. The two slaves to whom he had given the larger amounts of money immediately went to work, trying to increase their master's wealth. But the third servant was afraid of losing that with which he had been entrusted, so he hid it.

When the master returned, he found that the first two slaves had done well with their money, but the third had earned nothing with the talent he had been given. The first two were rewarded, and the third slave was punished.

The most common approach to this parable is that Jesus had given a treasure of great worth to his disciples, and then, after the Resurrection, Jesus would be going away for a time. The disciples did not know when Jesus would return, but they were supposed to use the gifts Jesus had given them to increase the kingdom while Jesus

---

Hiding money in ancient times was a common form of safekeeping. Coins from that time that have been unearthed largely came from such caches.

What treasure do you think Jesus gave to his disciples? With what has Jesus entrusted you? How are you using what Jesus has given to you?

> Why do you think Matthew was insistent that the disciples keep working while they waited? What implications does that have for us today?

was gone. Those who did what they were expected to do would be rewarded upon Jesus' return. Those who didn't do what was expected, even though they did not lose what Jesus gave them originally, would be punished when Jesus returned and required an accounting.

Matthew used this story is to keep the disciples working even though Jesus' return had been delayed. He admonished them not to lose focus, but to keep up their work for the kingdom.

Scenic Route

A couple of alternative ways of looking at this scripture passage involve a rethinking of the intentions of the third slave. The first has to do with the way the third slave viewed the master.

In this interpretation, we continue to think of the master as Jesus. The first two slaves took what was given to them and they invested quickly, trusting that their master cared for them and had their best interests at heart. They obviously wanted to do their best for their master, and their willingness to serve the master seems to indicate that they had found him to be good and generous. Because of their faithfulness, the master rewarded them with more.

> How might you have handled this situation as the master? the slaves?

The third slave viewed the master as a harsh taskmaster who created gain for himself where he does not even invest, which frightened the slave. Rather than risk losing the money, he hid it for safekeeping. When the slave reported to the master upon his return, the master was angry. As he pointed out, the slave could have at least invested the money. Interest rates were very high at that time and the master could have expected close to a 100 percent return on the investment. However, because the slave was afraid of using the money, he lost that with which he had been entrusted.

> What gifts are you afraid to use? Why?

In considering the third slave, we may wonder why two of the three slaves trusted the master, but the third feared him. It also causes us to wonder if the third slave misunderstood the master's intent in giving him the money. After all, the parable does not say that the master told the slaves to invest the money.

Whether we see Jesus as kind and generous or as harshly judging, we are right if we use this interpretation of the parable. Perhaps it challenges us to think of Jesus in different ways.

> How is it possible that Jesus is both generous and forgiving as well as harsh and judging?

There is yet another possible way of looking at this parable, and it questions the other two readings in their entirety. To read it this third way, we have to keep from associating the master with God or with Jesus or with any type of goodness. The master was a worldly man who was concerned only with material wealth. The first two slaves were rewarded because they made money for the master. The third slave was unwilling to enter into the earthly ways of using money to make money from others or even lending his money on interest.

When read in this way, the third slave was the only one who refused to conform to the ways of the world, for which he paid a price. In other places in the Gospel, Jesus asserted that those who do not conform to the ways of the world will pay a price. Could that be the message of this parable?

How might the third slave have been courageous by faithfully refusing to enter into the ways of the world's wealth?

Workers Ahead

Given the different ways of interpreting this parable, we have a sort of dilemma. On the one hand, we are called to use the talents we have been given to grow the kingdom. If we don't use our talents, they will wither and die or be given to others. We must not be afraid to venture beyond what we know and feel to be safe. There are tremendous rewards to be had by going beyond what is safe.

On the other hand, we may recognize that the economy of ancient Palestine rewarded the rich with more while taking away even the small amount that a poor person has. The same could be said of today. These realities are a part of the message that Jesus gave, and both need to be attended to by those who would follow Jesus.

Probably the easiest way to solve this dilemma is to say that we are to grow the things of heaven and not abuse the material things of the earth that may cause others to be in need, but the reality is usually much more complicated. Daily we have to count how we are using our gifts, including our abilities, efforts, time, and money. Daily we have to consider how our actions are building the kingdom of God or how they may be denying others of their daily bread. We have to be attentive to this reality, realizing that it isn't an easy answer. We are called to do our very best with what we have. Sometimes answers as to how to do that are unclear or even messy, but we must try to discern in each instance how Christ intends us to use our talents.

What might be gained by venturing beyond what is safe? When have you done so? What was the outcome?

"In English we commonly say that people have received talents of music, business acumen, leadership, and the like. That use of the word is derived from this parable" (*The Interpreter's Bible, Vol. 7*, ©1951, page 559).

When have you had to try to balance the investment of your own gifts with the well-being of others? How does a capitalist society affect your ability to do so?

How can you best use your gifts so that all may be uplifted?

In the Rear View

In this lesson we have looked at the parable of the talents through multiple lenses. Each of these lenses has something to tell us about how we should operate in the world. It is sometimes hard to determine how to use our gifts. If we use them to create growth, we must evaluate and be certain that the growth is for the kingdom of God, not for our own pockets or at the expense of others, especially the poor. That is a hard teaching to follow in modern society, but it is at the heart of what Jesus taught here and throughout his ministry.

Travel Log

Day 1:

What has the Master given you to use for the building of the kingdom? List your gifts/talents in the space below. Make a note about how you are using each one. Offer a prayer of thanks for these gifts and for the wisdom to use them well.

Day 2:

Look back over the list of gifts/talents you identified yesterday. What gifts are intended to be increased? What gifts might you be intended to give away for the sake of the kingdom?

Day 3:
   Draw a representation of Jesus. It doesn't have to be a literal drawing of a person. Maybe it is a cross or another symbol. Imagine yourself with Jesus. How do you envision Jesus—as a loving and generous master? as a harsh judge? somewhere in between? Why? Journal your thoughts in the space provided.

Day 4:
   Some people may equate the master leaving as God deserting the people/us. Rather than thinking of it in that way, consider the possibility that God has given you work to be done and the opportunity to make choices about how you do that work. For a considerable time, you have a fair amount of control. However, God will demand an accounting of your work. What did you waste by failing to use the talents God gave to you? by failing to increase that investment? by failing to venture beyond the safety of the known?
   Reflect on the questions and then write a prayer in which you ask God's forgiveness.

Day 5:
　Imagine yourself as the slave who received one talent. Why did you fear your master? Why were you not willing to venture beyond the safety of burying the money? What did you expect to happen when the master returned? How do you feel about your punishment?
　Compose a prayer for all of those who live in fear.

Day 6:
　Ponder the implications of this parable for those who continue to wait for Jesus' return. Make some notes about how you can work to be faithful while you continue to expect Jesus.

Day 7:
Write down your feelings about this parable. What is it really about? justice? grace? judgment? using our gifts? all these things?

A Solid Foundation

Scripture for lesson: Luke 6:39-42, 46-49

Before I was called into ministry, I planned to be a professional musician. Toward that end I earned both a bachelor's and a master's degree in music. My primary focus was classical voice. Although I was a voice major, I also had many classes on music theory and the history of what the academy would call "Western Music," which is basically music that is drawn from the European tradition.

One of the things I learned about music is that a sort of phenomenon began with the very earliest music and continues today. In the Baroque period this phenomenon was called the *basso continuo* or continuous bass. A group of instruments usually including a cello or string bass and a keyboard instrument such as the harpsichord provided this part of the music. In later music we might refer to it as the "rhythm section." You might think of a jazz band that has a bass, keyboard, and drums. These instruments serve as a foundation for the piece of music. Because they are keeping the beat, providing a basic harmony, and maintaining the bass line, singers or other instrumentalists are free to improvise.

A fundamental feature of music across the ages has been the importance of having a strong foundation upon which to build the rest of the sound. When that is missing, the music doesn't have the same feel, perhaps the same impact. Our lives are the same way. Without a foundation, we cannot do what is expected of us. Ultimately our work may simply become lost amidst the noise of the world.

What would music be like without its foundation?

Prep for the Journey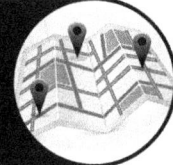

Today's parable is part of an extended sermon in the Gospel of Luke and follows on the heels of Luke's account of Jesus calling the Twelve from among his many followers. The first part of this sermon is quite similar to Matthew's account of Jesus delivering the Sermon

What do you think Jesus was trying to teach these newly chosen disciples about their role in his ministry? What do these teachings say to us as followers of Christ?

on the Mount. It is hard to say whether Matthew and Luke were recording the same event, or whether Jesus gave a similar sermon at a different time, with one sermon retold in Matthew's Gospel and the other appearing in Luke's.

As in the Sermon on the Mount, Luke's account includes Beatitude-like statements before moving into some parables that are actually more like proverbs. These statements can be very confusing. One bit of information that might help our understanding is that some scholars believe Jesus was using these teachings as a way of letting the newly chosen disciples know how he understood their relationship.

Read Luke 6:39-42.

He also told them a parable: "Can a blind person guide a blind person? Will not both fall into a pit? ⁴⁰ A disciple is not above the teacher, but everyone who is fully qualified will be like the teacher. ⁴¹ Why do you see the speck in your neighbor's eye, but do not notice the log in your own eye? ⁴² Or how can you say to your neighbor, 'Friend, let me take out the speck in your eye,' when you yourself do not see the log in your own eye? You hypocrite, first take the log out of your own eye, and then you will see clearly to take the speck out of your neighbor's eye.

"Discipleship means following someone who knows the way; as a result one becomes like the guide.…By following Jesus the disciples are implying that he is no blind guide but knows the way" (*The Cambridge Bible Commentary: The Gospel According to Luke*, E.J. Tinsley, © 1965, page 72). Continuing in that same vein, Jesus talked about how a teacher is above a disciple. The teachers/religious leaders of the day were corrupt and unfit to serve as teachers of the people. Since the goal of being a disciple is to become like the teachers, those people who followed the corrupt leaders would become like them. Jesus was calling his disciples to a higher standard.

Jesus continued by warning the disciples not to judge. In his ministry, Jesus taught, but he did not judge others. Only when a disciple has removed the log from his own eye, discovering his own faults, will he be able to help others see theirs. Were the disciples above their master that they could judge others when he did not?

What teachings are hardest for you to hear directed at you? Which ones immediately cause you to think of other people first? Why?

On the Road

Jesus had been instructing his disciples about their relationship with him and what his expectations were of them. He concluded his sermon with a call to action and a final parable that gave them the foundation on which to build their lives.

Read Luke 6:46-49.

"Why do you call me 'Lord, Lord,' and do not do what I tell you? ⁴⁷ I will show you what someone is like who comes to me, hears my words, and acts on them. ⁴⁸ That one is like a man building a house, who dug deeply and laid the foundation on rock; when a flood arose, the river burst against that house but could not shake it, because it had been well built. ⁴⁹ But the one who hears and does not act is like a man who built a house on the ground without a foundation. When the river burst against it, immediately it fell, and great was the ruin of that house."

It was common for disciples to call their teacher master or lord. "Before His resurrection, Jesus was addressed with the Jewish title of honor, Rabbi ('teacher'…Luke always, and Matthew usually, translated this title into Greek as *kurios* (Lord).…The resurrection changed the respectful student/teacher relationship of the disciples with Jesus into the believers' servant/Lord relationship. The designation of Jesus as Lord in the Gospels (esp. in Luke) is an indication of this shift in relationship" (*Holman Bible Dictionary*, © 1991, page 890).

While the Twelve disciples were newly chosen, that doesn't mean they were not already followers of Jesus. From the start of his ministry, people began to follow Jesus so that they could hear him teach. However, it is very unlikely at this point in Jesus' ministry that any of the Jews had recognized him as the Messiah. They knew he was, at the very least, a powerful prophet. Since they had already been following and listening to him teach, Jesus seemed somewhat exasperated that his followers were not doing what he had told them.

We have all had the experience of talking with people who appeared to be listening intently, only to realize later that they had not actually heard a word we had said. Or of telling people how to do something only to have our words ignored. We might like to think that if we had actually been in the crowd, able to hear Jesus teach, we would have clung to every word. Many people probably did, but some were likely distracted, and still others thought they knew more than Jesus did.

Jesus used a metaphor to illustrate his point by comparing the building of one's life on solid teachings to those who build their homes on solid foundations. While the people knew that a strong foundation was important in building, they seldom made the effort to create that type of foundation—or really much of a foundation at all. It was difficult and expensive to dig a foundation. Their homes were built of rocks found nearby and mud bricks the people made. Consequently, it was necessary to build and rebuild houses, which seldom lasted more than one generation. Jesus' metaphor held meaning for his listeners because they had seen the effects of rain, floods, and wind on their homes.

"Jesus points to the need not only to listen to his words but also to act. The one who hears and acts is the builder who digs out a strong foundation for his house. When the river floods, the high waters burst against the house but do not disturb it. Likewise, actions of the

> When have you experienced the situation described here? How did you feel? What happened?

> From what is your foundation constructed? How solid is it?

How has your foundation helped you to withstand the storms of life?

In what areas does your foundation need to be strengthened? What will you set aside so that you can focus on strengthening it?

What actions is Jesus calling you to take?

disciple that are based on Jesus' words provide strength in time of distress. The parable does not identify what happens in the process of acting out Jesus' words, only the results. It is not the teachings alone, but the act of following these instructions, that forms a firm foundation for the disciple" (*Feasting on the Word, Year C, Vol. 1*, by Susan E. Hylen, © 2009, page 408).

Scenic Route

As in all hilly countries, the streams of Galilee rush down the hillsides during the rainy seasons, overflow their banks, and leave sediment in their wake. During the dry season, the water had receded, leaving a somewhat level area that might, to a stranger, appear to be a good place to build a home. It would be easier to build there rather than trying to do so on the rugged rock. "But the people of the land would know and mock the folly of such a builder, and he would pass (our Lord's words may possibly refer to something that had actually occurred) into a byword of reproach. On such a house the winter torrent had swept down in its fury, and the storms had raged, and then the fair fabric, on which time and money had been expended, had given way and fallen into a heap of ruins" (Dean Plumptre as quoted in http://biblehub.com/commentaries/pulpit/luke/6.htm [May 16, 2017]).

Because such a literal foundation was so uncommon, Jesus may also have been suggesting that not only is it difficult to make his words the foundation of our lives, but that relatively few people will be able to do so. That kind of work takes dedication. It takes digging into the words of Jesus and digesting them for ourselves. It takes a lot of effort to set aside the other things in our lives so that we can and will focus on understanding Jesus' words and following them with action.

Workers Ahead

We live in a society very different from that of Jesus' time. We have almost instant access to all kinds of information. We are constantly being told what to believe, whom to believe, and even how to interpret what we hear and read. Often as we attempt to sort through it all—including our efforts to understand scripture—we tend to look for a way to make the facts match what we already believe. So, how can you be certain that you are not being influenced by false teachers or incorrect information?

Read your Bible and test the ideas presented to you against the truth of the scripture. Use sources that you have found to be reliable previously. For instance, be careful about the websites you use because many of them are not backed by facts. Read the opinions of other people and then compare those ideas against scripture. Talk with your pastor and other Christians. While their ideas will differ about some things, at least you can engage in a dialog with others who have similar beliefs.

Jesus said that we are to hear his words and take action based on them. Many people have been affected by the catastrophic floods of recent years—some of them multiple times. Many people ask why people continue to live and/or rebuild in those areas. They may have nowhere else to go. If they own the property, it's not likely that anyone would want to buy it since it is known to flood, which means they wouldn't have funds to build somewhere else. Maybe it's the only property they can afford to rent. Consequently, they are caught in the cycle of flood and rebuild.

How can you be certain that you are building your life on Jesus' words?

How faithfully are you following Jesus' words? What other things influence your life?

How can you and/or your group reach out to people who are suffering as the result of flooding or other natural disasters? What are you willing to do to help break the cycle of flooding and rebuilding?

In the Rear View

This parable of the wise and foolish builders starts out as a very logical statement. We know that people who build a house on a strong foundation will have a secure home. "In this text, Jesus bruises our egos in order to correct our vision, teach us lessons of the heart, and fine-tune our practices of faith. This sermon is not for the meek, mild or squeamish, because it demands change. The result, however, of hearing these words and doing them, of putting them into practice, is a house that will withstand the winds of change, the tests of time, and the rising tides that will certainly come" (*Feasting on the Word, Year C, Vol. 1*, by Vaughn Crowe-Tipton, © 2009, page 409).

If we are to live as Jesus commanded, we must go back and relearn the principles Jesus taught. They must become the foundation upon which we build our lives. It isn't easy, but it is what our Lord and Savior has called us to do.

What might need to change in your life after examining this parable?

Travel Log

Day 1:

What are the foundations of your life? Take a moment to list them and why they are foundational to who you are.

Day 2:

Jesus said to take the log out of our own eyes before trying to remove the speck in someone else's eye. How can you sustain a practice of self-examination to see what is in your own eyes? Create a plan that will help you to remove the logs from your eyes.

Day 3:

As you work on the foundation of your life, you may have to dig deep to find the bedrock. What is in your life that you might have to dig up to get to that bedrock? How hard might it be to dig up things that you have long since buried? As you reflect on these questions, journal your responses below.

Day 4:

How stable is the house of faith that you are building? Write down a few examples of times that you have experienced hardship but have persevered. How have these times strengthened your foundation of faith?

Day 5:
　Chances are that you know someone who is struggling to build a solid foundation for his or her life. Write that person a note of encouragement, possibly including the scripture for this parable.

Day 6:
　When have you called Jesus "Lord, Lord!" but withheld your trust in him? What causes you to lack the faith to trust and follow him? How can you remove those things from your path? Make some notes about the actions you will take.

Day 7:
    Reflect about the wise and foolish builders. Think of as many things as you can that people can have as foundations of their faith, especially in this time. List some of those things. Then brainstorm how you can help others to build upon the foundation of Jesus' words just as you are doing now.

Eat, Drink, And Be Merry

Scripture for lesson: Luke 12:15-21

You might be somewhat like me. When our family moved into a new house almost four years ago, we were shocked at all the stuff we had. I was excited because our new house has a storage building in the backyard, and I was hopeful that we would be able to get a lot of the stuff that we had been storing in our one-car garage out of the house. I even thought we might be able to use our new garage for its intended purpose: parking cars.

As I imagine many of you have guessed, we filled up that storage building and now we have a two-car garage that is also full. Oh, and then there's the attic….

When I read the parable on which we will focus in this lesson, I think about the desire to build bigger storage buildings and bigger barns to store all the things that I want to keep. In some ways this is just a human phenomenon, but for the rich man in Jesus' story, I think we will find that there are some other underlying causes.

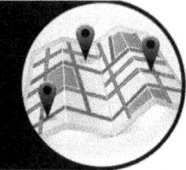

Prep for the Journey

It is important to place Jesus' teachings within their contexts. We are all aware that the same words spoken in a different time or setting can mean something different.

In the case of this parable, Jesus had just been eating at the home of a Pharisee who marveled that Jesus did not ceremonially wash before eating. Jesus used this opportunity to point out the hypocrisy of the Pharisees as a group. When a lawyer spoke up to say that Jesus' words were offensive, Jesus also spoke woe to lawyers for their own hypocrisy. Finally he went outside, and the Gospel tells us that there the Pharisees began to be very hostile toward him, cross examining him. Luke said that they were "lying in wait for him, to catch him in something he might say" (Luke 11:54).

> What do your storage areas look like? Are they clean and empty? Or are they bursting?
>
> Why do you choose to keep things? What influences your decision to keep something?
>
> How might the context of this parable change the way you understand it?
>
> Why do you think Jesus would choose to be so confrontational, especially when the confrontation was with the host at whose home he had been invited to have dinner?

As we discussed in an earlier lesson, the culture of Jesus' time was one of honor and shame. A contest arising from that perspective drew crowds, especially when the religious leaders were involved. Probably because the conversation was so contentious, the first verse of chapter twelve tells us, "Meanwhile, when the crowd gathered by the thousands, so that they trampled on one another, he began to speak first to his disciples…" Luke didn't report any change of scene, so it seems that he intended us to think this teaching took place outside the Pharisee's home in front of a large crowd that included many disciples and some of the Pharisees.

In the midst of this conversation, Jesus taught about being willing to stand up to those who had authority to kill and to be willing to defend themselves when they were brought before the authorities. While he was teaching, someone from the crowd called out to Jesus, asking him to arbitrate a family quarrel. It doesn't seem to have had much to do with the context, which causes one to wonder why this person raised the issue. However, his request, "Teacher, tell my brother to divide the family inheritance with me" (Luke 12:13b) gave Jesus the opportunity to teach using the parable we are about to read.

> What might cause you to "speak words of woe" to one or more groups of people in a very public venue?

> Why do you think this person came to Jesus about the dispute with his brother?

> How have you seen someone be affected by a situation similar to the dispute brought to Jesus? How was it resolved?

On the Road

Jesus' response to the person from the crowd in preparation for telling the parable is that people should be on guard against all kinds of greed. This is an interesting place for Jesus to start.

Read Luke 12:15-21.

And he said to them, "Take care! Be on your guard against all kinds of greed; for one's life does not consist in the abundance of possessions." ¹⁶ Then he told them a parable: "The land of a rich man produced abundantly. ¹⁷ And he thought to himself, 'What should I do, for I have no place to store my crops?' ¹⁸ Then he said, 'I will do this: I will pull down my barns and build larger ones, and there I will store all my grain and my goods. ¹⁹ And I will say to my soul, Soul, you have ample goods laid up for many years; relax, eat, drink, be merry.' ²⁰ But God said to him, 'You fool! This very night your life is being demanded of you. And the things you have prepared, whose will they be?' ²¹ So it is with those who store up treasures for themselves but are not rich toward God."

Scripture does not explicitly tell us that the person in the crowd was a man, but it seems likely, because of the request that was made. According to the law, a man's estate was to be divided among his sons, with the eldest son getting a double portion. If a man only had daughters, the property was to be divided among the daughters, but they were then required to marry someone from their own tribe so that the property would not move from one tribe to another. Unfortunately, there was no concept of gender equality at the time.

At first glance, it seems like this person in the crowd had a legitimate case. We, of course, do not know the details, but it is suggested that this man had an elder brother who was taking all of the inheritance. If that is the case, then his desire for help was understandable. He appealed to Jesus to help him receive what was his by law.

> Why do you think Jesus responded to the man as he did?

Rather than getting into the personal details, Jesus immediately warned people to be on guard against greed. The next statement explains why: "One's life does not consist in the abundance of possessions." True, these possessions may have been stolen, but the purpose of our existence is not to store up possessions for ourselves. The purpose of living is to serve God alone and trust in God to care for us.

> How do you feel about Jesus' response? Why?

Remember, Jesus had just been talking about being willing to give up one's life in faithfulness to God. Maybe because of what he had been teaching, this request to "help me get what is rightfully mine" was a bit frustrating. A jarring story was just what the people needed to get their minds on the things of God instead of the things of this world.

Scenic Route

Those who have ever raised crops, even a garden, know the wisdom of preserving the bountiful harvest of one year against the possible scarcity of the future. So, why did Jesus use this story to teach people about greed?

R. Alan Culpepper, Dean of the School of Theology at Mercer University in Atlanta offers five suggestions in the "Reflections" section of *The New Interpreter's Bible, Vol. IX* (© 1995, page 257). Each of these is ma be part of the reason Jesus felt negatively about this rich man, and each is likely a lesson we can learn from the rich man's behavior. The following information is based on Culpepper's statements.

Preoccupation with Possessions. The man in Jesus' story was completely focused on what he had and how much more he could get. He was so fixated on his own possessions that he did not what was happening around him. Remember, Jesus was responding to someone who had asked about his inheritance. It seems that Jesus was trying to show the questioner that he needed to change his focus from the things of the world to things that would last for eternity. Perhaps Jesus wanted him to consider the relationship he had with his family.

> What is likely to happen when a person becomes preoccupied with his or her possessions? How can a person avoid such a situation?

Security in Self-Sufficiency is perhaps one of the greatest heresies of our modern existence. We are taught from very early in our lives that we have the ability, if we are strong enough, smart enough, and persistent enough, to end our reliance on other people. Having everything we need to survive may be possible, but scripture and life experience teach us that we need relationships with God and others for true fulfillment.

The Grasp of Greed. Maybe because of his lack of companionship (there is no one else mentioned in the man's life or household) this man had no concept of the good that he could do for others. There were needy people during this time, just as there are needy people today. Apparently this man had such an abundance that he didn't even know what to do with it all. But his selfishness kept him from seeing the possibility of sharing. He was completely concerned with keeping all he had and making room for more.

Culpepper also points out that the man used the word *my* a lot. All those things belonged to him. He had no regard for whomever helped him to grow the crops or even for the abundance God had given him.

The Hollowness of Hedonism. The words the man used in this parable are one of the best examples of misquoting scripture. It is true that the words, "Eat, drink, and be merry," are in the Bible, but they are used in such a negative way that anyone who reads them knows that they are the opposite of what humans should do. Instead, we are to be willing to give to others, care for the poor, and if we are truly to be like Jesus, be willing to suffer in order to fulfill God's calling.

Practical Atheism is used to describe a life in which someone may claim to have known and followed God his or her whole life, but has remained unchanged by the words of scripture. "Sure," this man might have responded, "I believe in God. In fact, I've always believed in God," but it doesn't change his conduct. For all one could see in his life, he didn't know of God or the calls God has for loving others and caring for them.

As we think about this rich man and his abundant crop, it is hard not to think of our modern culture. Especially for those of us in the United States and other wealthy countries, we live in a world of excess. At the beginning of this study I mentioned all the possessions that our family has stored up in our home. I'm sure that many of you have the same type of situation in your homes.

Often we find ourselves with more than we need. John the Baptist told the people that if they had two coats they should give one away, and likewise if they had extra food, they should give it to someone

---

What are the positives and negatives of being self-sufficient?

How do you share what you have with those who are in need? How willing are you to accept what someone else wants to share with you?

How is practical atheism possible? Briefly share any instances of which you are aware.

Which of these five examples do you find to be the most important when considering the foolishness of this rich man?

Which ones might not apply? Why?

What would happen if we got out of the mindset of always wanting more? What would happen if we could simplify, and in that simplicity use the extra that we have for the well-being of those who are in need?

> What is necessary, and what is excess in your life? What do you intend to do about any excess?
>
> How can you address the issue of people in this land of plenty being chronically hungry? What might your faith community be willing to do?
>
> What would be necessary for this type of simplification in your life?

in need (Luke 3:11). People in our day and age are not good about sharing with those who have less. In fact, maybe as we have gained in abundance, we have become worse at sharing that abundance.

We must hear the words of Jesus and allow them to make a difference in our lives. We must hear his words and allow them to change us. Perhaps we could start by trying to determine what we need for our lives. Not what we want, but what we need. Anything above that is excess.

Our economy is based on companies and services competing for our excess. Whatever we have, we almost surely spend, because there always seems to be more comfort, more opportunity, more something that we should get to make ourselves feel better.

In light of rising food costs and the number of people in our country who are chronically hungry, some places have started community gardens. A plot of otherwise unused land, maybe in the midst of a city, is cultivated and people are allowed to use a portion of it to grow food. In other locations, people are invited to come in and harvest what is left after the majority of the crop has been picked. One small church buys seasonal foods at a low cost from area farmers, packages it and freezes it for distribution to people who are hungry during the winter months. Another rural church planted a garden and sent the produce into the city for distribution to people who otherwise would not have had access to fresh vegetables.

I think that Jesus would consider simplifying and sharing as being faithful to God. Setting aside greed and increasing compassion and relationship with others is what Jesus was all about.

In the Rear View

Jesus went from a confrontation with Pharisees to having a huge audience of people who were trampling each other to get to him. One in the crowd shouted out a request for help in regards to his inheritance. That request gave Jesus the opportunity to teach about greed and the impermanence of earthly wealth.

Our lives are an opportunity to live out that lesson. Doing so means we will be different from the people around us, but I believe Jesus wants us to take care of those who don't have enough.

Travel Log

Day 1:
   List the things you really need in order to live. As you look over the list, think about the places where you spend your money or time. How might you use your resources in a better way?

Day 2:
   Comfort and pleasure are two things that seem to motivate the rich man in this parable. All humans desire these things. Consider what you think is the right balance of comfort and pleasure as opposed to work or sacrificial giving in your life. Make some notes about your musings.

Day 3:

Imagine you are the person in the crowd who asked Jesus the question about his inheritance. What type of feelings might you have as Jesus tells this story? Write down the response you might have given if you'd had the chance.

Day 4:

Review the five suggested possibilities given for Jesus' critique of the rich man's actions. (See "The Scenic Route.") Which of these most pertains to you in your life right now? Write down the advice you would like to give to yourself about that issue.

Day 5:

Community seems to be one of the things missing from the rich man's life. Consider the various communities in your life. Of what communities are you a part? How strong are they? What is it like to be part of a strong community? a weaker community? How can you help others to be in community? Jot down some ideas as you consider the questions.

Day 6:

Jesus started this discourse by responding to the hypocrisy of the Pharisees. In some ways the entire conversation was about the hypocrisy of saying one was a follower of God and then being unwilling to trust in God or be faithful to God.

What might you say to this rich man if you could talk to him before he decided what to do with his abundance? How could you convince him of his hypocrisy? Outline the basis of your conversation with the rich man.

Day 7:
Most people look forward to a time in the future when they will be able to retire and enjoy the fruits of their labor. Many are putting away a portion of their salary now so that in the future they can relax and "enjoy life."

Take a moment to reflect about this process of saving for the future. How is it different from the actions of the rich man? How is it similar? Record some of your thoughts below.

A Reversal of Fortunes

Scripture for lesson: Luke 16:13-15, 19-31

A story has circulated about an incident that happened at a church probably not unlike many of our churches. According to the story, as people arrived for worship one Sunday, a person who appeared to be homeless was resting against the door of the church. Her clothes were dirty and ragged. As people made their way into the church, some stepped over her, and others even encouraged her to leave. No one offered to help, nor did they speak to her in a friendly manner.

Eventually the congregation gathered in the sanctuary, awaiting the beginning of the service, but the pastor did not appear to be present. A few minutes before the service was to start, the tension increased as to whether or not the pastor was coming that day. Just as the people were ready to start looking for the pastor, the homeless person who had been sitting outside came into the sanctuary.

The people groaned, thinking that she was going to ask for money, and they pondered the best way to address the situation. As the homeless person went down the center aisle, she slowly removed a hat, scarf, and other items that had hidden her identity. It became obvious before long that the homeless person was actually their pastor, who had dressed that way to make a point before preaching on the parable of the rich man and Lazarus.

This story may or may not have actually happened, but there is an element of truth that we can learn from it.

> How do you think the members of that congregation felt? How do you think the pastor felt? Why?

Prep for the Journey

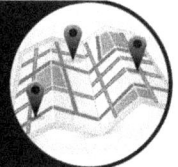

In the sixteenth chapter of his Gospel, Luke recorded some of Jesus' teachings about wealth. Luke, more than the other Gospel writers, showed sympathy for the poor. The birth stories tell of Jesus' humble beginnings and Luke's Gospel includes John the Baptist's teaching that people should share their possessions.

> Why might Luke have felt the need to share Jesus' teachings about wealth? Why do you think Luke was more sympathetic toward those who were poor?

Read Luke 16:13-15.

[Jesus said,] *"No slave can serve two masters; for a slave will either hate the one and love the other, or be devoted to the one and despise the other. You cannot serve God and wealth."*

14 The Pharisees, who were lovers of money, heard all this, and they ridiculed him. 15 So he said to them, "You are those who justify yourselves in the sight of others; but God knows your hearts; for what is prized by human beings is an abomination in the sight of God.

Jesus was not condemning wealth, but the love of wealth. He knew that wealth in and of itself was not evil, but that it often interfered with a person's relationship to God. Jesus saw that the Pharisees were using their influence and the prestige of their positions as leaders of the people to become rich, while other people, including many of those who followed him, had less than they needed. Against this backdrop, Jesus told the story of the rich man and Lazarus.

> **Why can a person not serve both God and wealth? What does this say about Christians who are wealthy?**

On the Road

At first glance, this story may seem easy to understand, but it actually has several layers of meaning. Some scholars think that Jesus was relating an actual incident, but others insist that it was a parable. Regardless of whether it was an actual incident or a parable, Jesus knew that it "must be striking and memorable, so that as the story is retold and remembered, the spiritual truth is reinforced again and again. The hearers must be able to imagine the situation" (http://www.jesuswalk.com/lessons/16_19-31.htm [May 22, 2017]).

> **What difference does it make to you as to whether this story actually happened or was a parable?**

Read Luke 16:19-21.

"There was a rich man who was dressed in purple and fine linen and who feasted sumptuously every day. 20 And at his gate lay a poor man named Lazarus, covered with sores, 21 who longed to satisfy his hunger with what fell from the rich man's table; even the dogs would come and lick his sores.

As his audience would have expected, Jesus began by talking about the rich man. He was a person whom society would have recognized as being important. Jesus enhanced the image of the man's wealth by mentioning that he was wearing purple clothing made from fine linen, both of which were indicative of luxury. Purple dye was very expensive, and the Romans had even established rules about who could wear purple and how much of the color they were to wear. Jesus further established the man's wealth by mentioning that he feasted every day. Most people were fortunate if they had a meal that included meat once a week, much less a daily feast.

> **What things would indicate a person's wealth in today's world? How clear are the differences between those who are wealthy and those who are poor?**

Lazarus, which means "one whom God helps," would have been at the very bottom of society's ladder. "Lazarus' condition is exactly opposite that of the rich man. He is sick—covered with sores. He is hungry—longing for the scraps from the rich man's table. At banquets, people wipe grease from their hands onto a piece of bread and then throw the bread on the floor. To long for such soiled bread is the height of misery—of degradation" (https://www.sermonwriter.com/biblical-commentary/luke-1619-31 [May 22, 2017]), yet Lazarus would gladly have eaten those scraps of food.

Lazarus was about as poor and sick as one could imagine. He lay at the gate, which suggests that he didn't even have the strength to sit or stand, and which is further suggested by the comment that the dogs licked his sores. At that time, dogs were street animals and considered to be unclean. The contemporary image of a pet offering comfort to a suffering person would have been foreign to the people of Jesus' day. Surely if Lazarus had been able to move or defend himself, he would have shooed away the dogs.

The rich man was not intentionally cruel to Lazarus. In fact, he may have thought he was being kind by not having the poor beggar moved from his gate. He could have had the servants give Lazarus some of the table scraps, but he did not truly see Lazarus. "He was too absorbed in himself to be able to see. He was a man of large affairs, and there were problems galore connected with his house and estate; and soon [he] was so close to himself that he could not see Lazarus, though the beggar was as near as the doorstep" (*The Interpreter's Bible, Vol. 8*, © 1952, page 291). It was as if Lazarus had become part of the landscape, something the rich man expected to see, but did not truly notice.

> How could the rich man not have noticed Lazarus? Whom do you fail to see?

Read Luke 16:22.
²² The poor man died and was carried away by the angels to be with Abraham. The rich man also died and was buried.

Given Lazarus' health, Jesus' audience would not have been surprised to learn that he died, but it would have surprised them to hear that the rich man had also died. In fact, both of them died about the same time. But in telling of their deaths, Lazarus was mentioned first. In the world, perhaps the rich man was superior, but at their deaths the tables had turned. Angels took Lazarus to be with Abraham, the father of the Jewish faith. The rich man was buried and ended up in Hades, where he endured torment. One received awful things in life, but was rewarded in the afterlife; the other received wonderful things in life, but was punished in the afterlife.

> How do you view the afterlife? What things have influenced your view?

> Which of these two men would you rather be? Why?

Read Luke 16:23-26.
In Hades, where he was being tormented, he looked up and saw Abraham far away with Lazarus by his side. ²⁴ He called out, 'Father Abraham, have mercy on me, and send Lazarus to dip the tip of his finger in water and cool my tongue; for I am in agony in these flames.'

> When have you witnessed a reversal of fortunes? What was your reaction to the situation?

> How do you feel about the rich man's request to send Lazarus on errands? Why?

> In what ways do you find comfort from this parable? How might it offer comfort to others?

> How are you like the family of the rich man? What must you do about it?

^{25} *But Abraham said, 'Child, remember that during your lifetime you received your good things, and Lazarus in like manner evil things; but now he is comforted here, and you are in agony. ^{26} Besides all this, between you and us a great chasm has been fixed, so that those who might want to pass from here to you cannot do so, and no one can cross from there to us.'*

The reversal of their situations became clear when the rich man looked across a chasm and saw Lazarus with Abraham, the father of the Jewish faith. This conversation is almost certainly only for the purposes of this story and to show us the rich man's heart. There is no other indication that this type of communication is possible between those in torment and those gaining a reward after death.

The rich man, seeing that Lazarus had been rewarded, seemed to think that things were still the same as they had been when he was alive: He was still rich and powerful, and Lazarus was lowly. The rich man asked Abraham to send Lazarus to ease his suffering. Even though the rich man apparently had done little for Lazarus, he felt he could ask Lazarus to be his servant. When Abraham reminded him that their situations had changed, the rich man still wanted Abraham to send Lazarus to warn his brothers of what was to come so that they would repent. It may be touching that he thought of someone other than himself in this moment, but he still seemed to think very little of Lazarus.

Verse 26 "puts Abraham, the parent of faith, in the role of judge. Abraham sits with Lazarus, indicating a startling truth about who is faithful and who is not. What we know from the parable is that because of his lack of action and compassion, the rich man cannot cross over to the place of faith, nor does he have a place by Abraham's side. To an impoverished group of people, this parable would offer great comfort that God sees their suffering and is on their side" (*Feasting on the Word, Year C, Vol. 4*, by G. Penny Nixon, © 2010, page 121).

Read Luke 16:27-31.

He said, 'Then, father, I beg you to send him to my father's house— ^{28} for I have five brothers—that he may warn them, so that they will not also come into this place of torment.' ^{29} Abraham replied, 'They have Moses and the prophets; they should listen to them.' ^{30} He said, 'No, father Abraham; but if someone goes to them from the dead, they will repent.' ^{31} He said to him, 'If they do not listen to Moses and the prophets, neither will they be convinced even if someone rises from the dead.'"

In telling parables, the purpose is that those who hear them will be able to identify with one or more of the characters or situations. In this parable, we are more likely to identify with the family of the rich man who was left behind. We have wealth, especially in comparison to the residents of many countries. Often, we want a sign—something or someone to prove the truth of a situation to us. Accepting things we are told, sometimes even things we have seen, is difficult. "Even if Lazarus returned, the brothers would have to believe that this really was Lazarus, that he really had died, and that he really had a message from their brother" (*Feasting on the Word, Year C, Vol. 4*, by Scott Bader-Saye, © 2010, page 120).

Some scholars believe that "the rich man and his brothers represent the unbelieving Jews. Jesus is made to assert that they have stubbornly refused to repent in spite of the obvious testimony to himself in Scripture and to predict that they will fail to be impressed by his resurrection" (The Interpreter's Bible, Vol. 8, c 1952, page 289). As with the brothers, their only hope was to hear the words of the prophets and allow their lives to be changed.

> How do you feel about the comparison of the brothers to the unbelieving Jews? In what ways is it an accurate/inaccurate comparison?

Scenic Route

Lazarus is the only name Jesus ever gave to a character in one of his parables. It has been suggested by some scholars that Jesus either knew or had heard about a man named Lazarus who had suffered this kind of fate. Surely Jesus knew people who were sick and starving; maybe one of them was named Lazarus.

In Jesus' time, wealth was considered to be a blessing from God, and poverty was a curse from God. But the only one given a name was probably the poorest, sickest, and lowest member of society. Perhaps Jesus was making a statement to the world. Jesus knows all people. Jesus regards all people as worthy of love and as worthy of adoption into the kingdom of God. Jesus especially knows those whom everyone else has forgotten. He knows their story. He knows their hearts. He knows their names.

> Who are the people in your life whose names you don't know or whose stories you don't know fully? How do you think Jesus would suggest you treat those people?

Workers Ahead

"This text presents us with the great moral challenge of seeing, and then making visible, the invisible suffering of the world. Indeed, this may be one of our most important moral challenges today. Our global network of communication allows us to be more aware of the world's suffering than ever before, but we have become adept at ignoring the suffering that is right at our doorstep" (*Feasting on the Word, Year C, Vol. 4*, by Scott Bader-Saye, © 2010, pages 116, 118).

Jesus said that the poor would always be with us. I don't believe things are supposed to be that way, but that Jesus knew there would

> What suffering is happening at your doorstep? What are you doing alleviate that suffering?

always be rich people who dressed in purple among us, too. As long as the world has those who consume and hoard more than they need, others will have less than they need.

Jesus also taught that we would be judged by how we treat and care for the least of these. Sometimes it is hard for us to get involved in caring for those in need. Maybe we are afraid or overwhelmed. The rich man in this parable, however, had the opportunity to care for someone. He passed by him every day. He even knew his name. He must have known that right there, at his own gate, a man was starving to death, but he chose to ignore that man.

Poverty, need, homelessness, and many other ills of our world may seem like insurmountable problems. When we look at these problems in their wholeness, they are overwhelming. Like the rich man in this parable, we should instead notice the needs of those around us. Maybe God is placing in our paths right now people who need something of which we have an abundance.

> What might you have an abundance of that someone else could use?
>
> What person in need has been placed in your path?

In the Rear View

Jesus dealt with issues surrounding wealth in this set of teachings. He taught that we cannot serve both God and money. He criticized those who loved money, which included the Pharisees. Then he told a story about a very wealthy man who watched as a poor man died of starvation. In death, the poor man was rewarded, but the rich man was tormented.

The question remains for those of us somewhere on the spectrum between these two extremes: How will we use our wealth to help others? Albert Schweitzer seems to have summed it up well: "Even if it's a little thing, do something for those who have need of a man's help, something for which you get no pay but the privilege of doing it."

> What will you do for someone today? How can you influence others to share with others as well?

Travel Log

Day 1:

In the space below, write the name of a Lazarus in your life. This may not be someone who is in desperate need, but someone who has a need that you may have the ability to fill. Write for a few moments about how you might fill his or her need.

Day 2:

Create two columns in the space below. At the top of one write wealth, and at the top of the other write God. Under these headings, list ways that you pursue each one. Review your list, and pray about it.

Day 3:

Take a short walk around your living space. Identify things that you haven't used in a while and then create a list of these items. What things do you really not need? Where might they be better used? How willing are you to part with your excess so others may have a more fulfilled life?

Day 4:

Imagine yourself as one of the disciples listening as Jesus told this story. Remember that the crowd around you includes both people who are rich and those who are poor. What are you thinking as Jesus says these words? Journal your thoughts and reactions.

Day 5:

At this point in your life, you still having the ability to choose your own fate, as did the rich man's brothers. What changes do you need to make so that you can follow the words of the prophets? Make some notes as to how you will improve as a follower, especially in relation to caring for the poor, widows, orphans, and the imprisoned.

Day 6:

Put yourself in the place of the Pharisees. How might you react to Jesus questioning you and pointing out your richness? How might you defend yourself? How would people today defend themselves in a similar situation? Write a prayer asking God to forgive you for those times when you have fallen short of what was needed. Also ask God to give you opportunities to minister to others.

Day 7:
Review the list you created the first day of this week. As you have considered other things about this lesson, who can you add to that list? Pray over your list and your plan to care for someone in your own path.

They Know His Voice

Scripture for lesson: John 10:1-18

Just this past week I had one of those experiences that re-orients your brain to think of something in a new way. I have been trying to learn Spanish. I have learned quite a bit over the years, but whenever I get in a conversation, something freezes, and I can't quite get up to speed. So, I use Google Translate.

In planning a meeting with a Spanish-speaking candidate for the ministry from my presbytery, I received a text. I was pretty sure I got the meaning, but just to make sure, I ran the message through Google Translate.

This candidate is very polite and always addresses me as "pastor." That was one of the words I was pretty sure I understood in the text, but when I viewed the translation, Google thought I had been addressed as "shepherd."

In the back of my mind, I know how closely related those words are. But here was another reminder that when I take on the role of "pastor," I am really taking on the role of "shepherd." That role is different from other ways in which a minister may serve. In my mind, being a shepherd is one of the most important things a minister can do.

Even having said that, I realize that as a minister I am never truly the shepherd. At my installation as pastor of the First Cumberland Presbyterian Church in Murfreesboro, the Rev. Dr. Perryn Rice challenged me to be a good sheep dog for the real shepherd, Jesus the Christ.

> In what roles does your minister(s) serve? Which role do you feel is the most important? Who decides how the minister's time is divided between the various roles in which he or she is asked to serve?

Prep for the Journey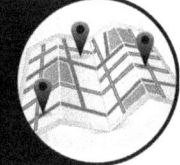

The original texts of Bible were not divided into chapters and verses. Those divisions were added to make it easier to find small portions of scripture. We have become so accustomed to this system that we sometimes don't realize that the text was not written that way.

> **How do you feel about Jesus' response the man was born blind so that others could experience the power of God? Why?**
>
> **Why would it have been difficult to take a stand against the Pharisees? What about the man's account of his healing might have caused the most concern for the Pharisees?**
>
> **Why do you think the Pharisees threw the man out of the Temple? How difficult would it have been for the man to continue to live among the same people after being thrown out of the Temple?**
>
> **What might cause a person to be thrown out of a church today? How do you feel about such actions?**

The section with which this lesson deals begins with the first verse of chapter 10, but it is a commentary on the events in the previous chapter. If we aren't careful, we may miss the context for the words that Jesus shared.

In chapter 9 Jesus encountered a man who had been blind since birth. At that time, physical limitations (such as being blind or lame) and diseases were thought to be a punishment from God for some wrongdoing—committed either by the person or the person's parents. With that in mind, the disciples asked Jesus why the man had been born blind. Jesus explained that his blindness was not due to any sin, but was so that they could experience the power of God.

Jesus made some mud with his saliva, put the mud on the man's eyes, and told him to go and wash. After the man washed, he could see! As the story of this encounter circulated, the people wanted to know how this man who had been blind from birth could now see. Some people didn't believe it was the same man, since that sort of thing never happened and seemed impossible.

The Pharisees inserted themselves into the interrogation. They wanted to know who this man was, and they wanted proof that he had been born blind. The Pharisees also demanded to know who had healed him as well as when and how. It might seem normal to us that the Pharisees would have wanted to know all of these things. With this information, they could possibly have helped others who were blind. They might even have been able to partner with Jesus so as to serve God's people better together. Or they might even simply have been curious. Of course, we know that their motives were not that honorable.

As the Pharisees investigated this miracle more closely, they kept finding things with which they took issue. They were upset because the healing had taken place on the Sabbath, and because it constituted work. It was against the law to perform any type of work on the Sabbath, and the Pharisees were all about keeping the law. They were upset because the healed man had called Jesus a prophet, which gave him more credence with the people. They were upset that the man had reverence for Jesus when they felt he should have had more reverence for them. After all, they were the religious leaders and interpreters of the law. The man even had the audacity to suggest that the Pharisees might also want to become disciples of the One who had healed him.

Eventually, the Pharisees threw the previously blind man out of the Temple. Because the Jewish faith is also a way of life, not only did their action keep him from offering sacrifices and participating in worship or feasts, but it also separated him from the rest of the community.

On the Road

Jesus was frustrated with the Pharisees' reaction to the healing of the man who had been blind from birth and so used this opportunity to talk about judgment and spiritual blindness. Some Pharisees who happened to be nearby said, "Surely, we are not blind, are we?" Jesus responded that for those who remained blind, their sin was not counted against them, but for those who said they could see, their sin remained.

At this point Jesus started to talk about the sheep, the gate, and the shepherd. There are several metaphors in this parable. The images are different enough that some scholars have suggested that the story is actually two parables, but regarding it as one parable with multiple images is probably a better way to examine it. At the first part of the parable, Jesus referred to himself as the gate of the sheepfold.

Read John 10:1-10.

"Very truly, I tell you, anyone who does not enter the sheepfold by the gate but climbs in by another way is a thief and a bandit. ² The one who enters by the gate is the shepherd of the sheep. ³ The gatekeeper opens the gate for him, and the sheep hear his voice. He calls his own sheep by name and leads them out. ⁴ When he has brought out all his own, he goes ahead of them, and the sheep follow him because they know his voice. ⁵ They will not follow a stranger, but they will run from him because they do not know the voice of strangers." ⁶ Jesus used this figure of speech with them, but they did not understand what he was saying to them.

⁷ So again Jesus said to them, "Very truly, I tell you, I am the gate for the sheep. ⁸ All who came before me are thieves and bandits; but the sheep did not listen to them. ⁹ I am the gate. Whoever enters by me will be saved, and will come in and go out and find pasture. ¹⁰ The thief comes only to steal and kill and destroy. I came that they may have life, and have it abundantly.

It was common for shepherds to join together for protection and companionship when they had to take their flocks to distant areas to find grazing land. They built an enclosure and put all of the sheep together at night. The role of gatekeeper probably rotated between the shepherds. The enclosures or sheepfolds had one gate, so the only persons who had legitimate access to the sheep were the ones the gatekeeper allowed through the gate. Thievery was a common problem for shepherds, which was one reason for putting the sheep in an enclosure with limited access. Of course, wild animals also preyed upon the flocks.

You may wonder how the shepherds were able to separate their flocks when they took the sheep out to graze. Sheep recognize their

> How do you interpret Jesus' statement about blindness, sight, and sin?

> What current example might parallel Jesus' use of the gate and the sheepfold?

shepherd's voice and will only follow that person. Therefore, when the shepherd called, only his sheep responded and followed him out of the sheepfold.

Then Jesus said, "All who came before me are thieves and bandits…," which seems a rather odd statement for him to have made. We know from many of Jesus' other sayings that he had great regard for the prophets of the Old Testament. In fact, he often lamented the people's rejection of those messengers from God. So, it is unlikely that Jesus' reference included the prophets. It is more likely that Jesus was referring to passages like Ezekiel 34 in which the kings of Israel were leading the people astray while the prophets attempted to set them back on the right path. By Jesus' time, the Pharisees and other religious leaders had become the thieves and bandits. Their leadership was not in the best interest of God's people.

Sometimes we skip this part and go straight to Jesus' identification of himself as the good shepherd, but the gate is an important image. Jesus is the only way for the sheep and the shepherd to be united. Even if others manage to gain access, the sheep know their shepherd and will not go with anyone else.

Scenic Route

In the second half of this parable, Jesus changed the way in which he referred to himself. Instead of being the gate for the sheep, Jesus identified himself as the shepherd.

Read John 10:11-18.

"I am the good shepherd. The good shepherd lays down his life for the sheep. [12] The hired hand, who is not the shepherd and does not own the sheep, sees the wolf coming and leaves the sheep and runs away—and the wolf snatches them and scatters them. [13] The hired hand runs away because a hired hand does not care for the sheep. [14] I am the good shepherd. I know my own and my own know me, [15] just as the Father knows me and I know the Father. And I lay down my life for the sheep. [16] I have other sheep that do not belong to this fold. I must bring them also, and they will listen to my voice. So there will be one flock, one shepherd. [17] For this reason the Father loves me, because I lay down my life in order to take it up again. [18] No one takes it from me, but I lay it down of my own accord. I have power to lay it down, and I have power to take it up again. I have received this command from my Father."

In another of Jesus' "I AM" statements, Jesus identified himself as the shepherd for the sheep. In the first half of this parable, God seems to have been the shepherd. One of the important aspects of John's

---

Sidebar:

Who are the bandits and thieves, those who would lead the sheep astray, in our world? How do you recognize your shepherd's voice?

What does it mean for Jesus to be the gate for the sheep? How does the image of Jesus as the gatekeeper speak to you?

Gospel is the reverence for Jesus as a divine figure. In this section of the parable, Jesus confirmed his own identity as being one with God.

But Jesus went even further. He had already identified himself as the good shepherd, but then he went on to explain what a good shepherd is. A good shepherd will give his life for the sheep. When the wolves come to steal the sheep, the good shepherd will fight to protect the sheep, even if it means losing his own life.

A hired hand won't give his life for the sake of the sheep. He has simply been hired to look after them. To the hired hand, the caring for the flock is just a job, a way to earn a living. The shepherd has a personal investment with the sheep. The good shepherd, the one who really cares for and knows the sheep, is willing to give his own life for their safety and welfare.

In both sections of the parable, knowledge of the sheep by the shepherd is important. Jesus truly knows his sheep, and they know his voice. Because of that relationship, Jesus is willing to give his life for them.

> For what or for whom would you be willing to lay down your life?
>
> How are the shepherds in your life like Jesus? like a hired hand?

Workers Ahead

Jesus made a striking claim in this parable. While the meaning is similar to the words Jesus used in other places, the change is important. Jesus said that not only did he have the power to lay down his own life, but he had power to take it up again. In other places, New Testament writers said that God raised Jesus on the third day. Jesus said that he had the power to rise again. No one else needed to do this for him, he would do it himself.

Over the centuries, many people have said that John's Gospel makes it clearer than do the others that Jesus was to be considered one with God. The basis for our understanding of the Holy Trinity may well be in this high reverence for Jesus.

As we take this parable into our modern lives, we need to be careful about a couple of things. First, Jesus told us that his sheep would hear his voice and follow him. He also said that when his sheep hear another voice they will run from it. We should be careful to whom we listen, especially in our modern world where so many voices compete for our attention.

Second, we should be careful when we consider ourselves to be shepherds. Jesus seems to suggest that anyone who considers themselves a shepherd is a thief or a bandit. I tend to think of myself as a shepherd of God's people, but perhaps I should strive to be the best sheep dog I can be.

> How is Jesus' claim about being able to take up his own life again different from God raising Jesus from the dead?
>
> What voices might we mistake for the shepherd's voice?
>
> How can we best help to serve the shepherd without lifting ourselves to a place where we don't belong?

In the Rear View

In this lesson we have discovered that the jumping off point for Jesus' statements about being the gate and the good shepherd was the discussion that followed the healing of the man who was blind from birth. Jesus then showed the Pharisees and other religious leaders to be thieves and bandits. They wanted to lead the people, but because they did not know the people, the people would not listen to or follow them.

Jesus then identified himself as the gate for the sheep, giving access for the sheep to be united with the shepherd, and then as the good shepherd, who would guide and care for the people. He ultimately would be confirmed as the good shepherd by giving his own life for the sheep.

What does it mean for us, as the sheep, to be united with our shepherd?

Travel Log

Day 1:

What voices call to you? How do they affect who you are? Maybe some of the voices are from advertisements, work, school, family, or other parts of your life. What do you think the Good Shepherd is saying as he calls to you? Journal your responses.

Day 2:

Imagine yourself as a Pharisee at the beginning of this parable. The Pharisees asked Jesus if they were blind also, apparently expecting him to say that they weren't. But Jesus' answer confirmed that they were. In what ways do you think the Pharisees were blind? How are you blind? How are those who seek to be shepherds today blind? As you reflect on the questions, doodle some responses.

Day 3:

What does the image of Jesus as the gate say to you about who Jesus is and who you are meant to be? Ponder this question for a few moments and list some of the ways the image of Jesus as the gate affects the ways in which you live out your faith.

Day 4:

What does it mean in your life to run from the thieves and bandits who try to distract you from the voice of the shepherd? How can you more effectively "run from" those thieves and bandits? Jot down some responses.

Day 5:

What does being united with the shepherd mean to you? How do you see Jesus in that role? In what other ways have you tried to be united with the shepherd? Journal your responses.

Day 6:

Consider the image of the hired hand as portrayed in this parable. What have been your experiences of working with a hired hand? How do you sometimes treat others as if you were a hired hand? Why? Write a prayer in which you seek forgiveness for those actions.

Day 7:

Many churches use shepherd groups as a way of meeting members' pastoral needs. The congregation is divided into smaller groups and a shepherd is assigned to each group. The shepherds are to touch base regularly with the people in their group, visit during times of illness or a death, and so forth. Such groups can be quite effective, especially in larger congregations, if the right people are serving as the shepherds.

List the qualities necessary for a person to be a good shepherd in this sense. What happens when someone is not a good shepherd?

The Kingdom of Heaven Is Like…

Scripture for lesson:
    Matthew 13:31-33, 44-53

A movie from the early 1990s had some of us proudly sporting mullets, big hair, and other unfortunate fashion trends. I was just getting ready to graduate from high school when the movie City Slickers became a blockbuster hit.

The film was about a group of male friends who were experiencing their mid-life crises. As a break from their very corporate lives, they went to a dude ranch to help with a cattle drive. Over the course of the movie, these men had a life-changing experience as they learned how to ride, rope, and work together to drive cattle.

One feature of the film is the difficult old cowhand, Curly, played by veteran Western actor Jack Palance. Curly was a tough man, and he seemed to give Billy Crystal's character, Mitch, a hard time. At one point, they rode off together in search of a lost cow, and there was a suggestion that Curly was going to do something awful to Mitch.

During that ride, Curly offered to tell Mitch the secret of life. When Mitch asked what it is, Curly simply held up one finger. He gave no explanation, no qualification. It wasn't until near the end of the movie that Mitch realized what Curly had been telling him: The secret to life is one thing, and it is up to each person to determine for himself or herself what that one thing is.

> What do you think of Curly's assertion that the secret of life is one thing? What is that one thing for you?

Prep for the Journey

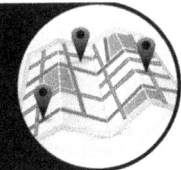

Most of us are interested in what the kingdom of heaven is like. We are curious without even really knowing what kinds of questions to ask. Sometimes when we think about the kingdom of heaven, we think primarily about the afterlife. We wonder what it will be like to live with God in heaven, whether the streets will really be gold, what our "mansions" will be like, and many other things like that. We look to scripture for clues about that eternal home.

> What do you think of when you imagine the kingdom of heaven?

119

What does the kingdom of heaven mean to you? How do you see the Church working to make the world like God's kingdom?

When Jesus talked about the kingdom of heaven, however, I think he meant something other than the eternal heaven where people will go when their lives on earth end. I think Jesus was referring to the way the world works, or at least the way the world will work, when God is fully in charge. Some people have described the kingdom of heaven as "already and not yet," meaning that the kingdom of heaven was introduced into the world through Jesus and his life on earth, but it has not become the way the world works because the final days have yet to come. For those who think about the kingdom of heaven in this way, one of the great purposes of the Church is to make the world as much like the kingdom of heaven as possible. We are to usher in the way God intends for the world to be.

On the Road

It would be great if Jesus had been specific about the way the kingdom of heaven works, but his sayings can seem confusing and hard to understand. One reason they seem that way may be so that people can reinterpret his words in the generations to come. We certainly read the words about the kingdom of heaven differently now than the first readers of Matthew's Gospel.

Another reason may be that the kingdom of heaven is so different from the way our world is structured that we can scarcely catch a glimpse of it. The best hope is to use figurative language, which is what Jesus did in these sayings.

Read Matthew 13:31-33.

He [Jesus] put before them another parable: "The kingdom of heaven is like a mustard seed that someone took and sowed in his field; ^{32} it is the smallest of all the seeds, but when it has grown it is the greatest of shrubs and becomes a tree, so that the birds of the air come and make nests in its branches."

^{33} He told them another parable: "The kingdom of heaven is like yeast that a woman took and mixed in with three measures of flour until all of it was leavened."

Why do you think Jesus' words about the kingdom can be difficult to understand?

These first two parables in Jesus' continuing discussion of the kingdom of heaven are surprising in several ways. In each story, the kingdom is compared to the total of the items and the outcome of their use. The mustard seed is part of the story, but the full story has to do with it being planted, its eventual size, and its ability to be a home for birds.

Many of us have learned about and perhaps even seen a mustard seed. Often they are given at retreats or conventions to help participants remember to have a "mustard seed" of faith. It is a tiny seed, much smaller than the seeds used to grow crops or even herbs. It is an extremely large plant, especially considering the size of the seed from which it grows.

Some sources have suggested that the tree Jesus described is similar to an imperial family tree, which has a strict power structure that started with one person. (For an example of an imperial family tree, visit https://en.wikipedia.org/wiki/Japanese_imperial_family_tree.) But the mustard plant is not like that. Perhaps one of the surprises about the kingdom of heaven is that it will provide a place where birds can nest.

The second saying about yeast is even a bit more surprising. In the Gospel of Matthew, Jesus warned the disciples to be wary of the "yeast of the Pharisees and Sadducees" (Matthew 16:6). Most of Jesus' references to yeast seem to be negative—with the exception of this one. But again, the story isn't just about yeast. By itself, yeast won't do anything. For yeast to serve its purpose, it must be mixed with other ingredients. In this example, a woman mixed the yeast with three measures of flour, which would have been enough to make bread for over a hundred people.

It seems like, as in the story of the mustard seed, the abundance of the amount produced by a small start was the point. Mixing yeast with a huge amount of flour until it is all leavened is like the kingdom of heaven, perhaps because that kingdom will be one of great abundance and surprising excess.

Scenic Route

This next group of sayings about the kingdom of heaven also seems to have something in common. But this time the kingdom of heaven is described so differently that it is hard to make a close connection between the first two sayings and the ones discussed in the following section.

Read Matthew 13:44-46.

"The kingdom of heaven is like treasure hidden in a field, which someone found and hid; then in his joy he goes and sells all that he has and buys that field.

⁴⁵ "Again, the kingdom of heaven is like a merchant in search of fine pearls; ⁴⁶ on finding one pearl of great value, he went and sold all that he had and bought it.

When I read this first story, I am almost always distracted by a legal and ethical question: Was it lawful for this person, who apparently

---

What does the size of the mustard plant mean in the parable?

Why do you think Jesus used "yeast" as a part of the kingdom of heaven here when it was used negatively in other places?

What does the need for human interaction with the seed and yeast say to you?

> How do you feel about the ethics of the man who discovered the hidden treasure? Why? Why do you think Jesus didn't address that part of the scenario in his teaching?
>
> In what ways is the image of a great treasure appropriate for the kingdom of heaven? How does it limit our understanding of the kingdom?

was plowing a field that belonged to someone else, to hide a treasure he found and then go buy the field without disclosing the treasure to the owner? Even if it was legal, was it an ethical thing to do? Jesus ignored this question entirely, probably because the point had nothing to do with that distraction.

Scholars feel certain that the man was poor, especially because he was plowing someone else's land. Just imagine stumbling across a buried treasure! "In Palestine, long subject to invasion, such discoveries were not unknown. Somebody buried the money at a time of threat, was killed or exiled; and then, perhaps years later, the blade of some poor plowman unearthed it" (*The Interpreter's Bible, Vol. 7*, © 1951, page 419). Without looking for it, this man found a treasure beyond his wildest dreams. He recognized its value for him and for his life. It was so valuable, in fact, that he was willing to sell everything that he had in order to have the treasure.

Jesus wanted people to understand that the kingdom of heaven is worthy of our willingness to give up everything so that we can have it. The kingdom is the one thing for which we should strive above all other things, and it is the one thing worth every other thing we have.

The second story is similar in some ways, but there are subtle differences. This merchant had been looking for pearls. We may even think that he has gone all over, searching for the one pearl that was so perfect, so wonderful, that his entire collection would seem trivial in comparison.

> How have you seen people search for that perfect pearl? How successful were their efforts?

Even though this merchant had been looking for such a pearl, he still seemed surprised when he found it. It was greater than he had imagined it would be. It was so wonderful, in fact, that everything else he had was no longer of any importance. He knew that he must have that one pearl, even at the cost of everything else he had.

> For what would you be willing to give up all of your worldly possessions? Why?

Jesus suggests that we must be willing to give up everything we have in order to attain the kingdom of heaven. Whether we are seeking the kingdom with all our hearts or simply plowing in the field, when we find the kingdom (or maybe when it finds us), we must be willing to give up whatever else we have that has value to us so that we can be a part of that kingdom. Treasure is an easy word to explain the kingdom, but it is imperfect, because it implies worldly value. The kingdom of heaven is available to those who will give up their love or desire for the values of the world.

> What are you treasures?

Workers Ahead

The first of these two stories is a warning. Jesus had told the people what was important and given them examples of how the kingdom of heaven could come from a small beginning, yet grow into something different and much larger. Jesus had also told his listeners that the kingdom of heaven was worth giving up all one had to obtain it. As if those two messages weren't enough, Jesus ended this discourse with examples of what the kingdom of heaven will be like when it comes to its fullness.

Read Matthew 13:47-53.

"Again, the kingdom of heaven is like a net that was thrown into the sea and caught fish of every kind; 48 when it was full, they drew it ashore, sat down, and put the good into baskets but threw out the bad. 49 So it will be at the end of the age. The angels will come out and separate the evil from the righteous 50 and throw them into the furnace of fire, where there will be weeping and gnashing of teeth.

51 "Have you understood all this?" They answered, "Yes." 52 And he said to them, "Therefore every scribe who has been trained for the kingdom of heaven is like the master of a household who brings out of his treasure what is new and what is old." 53 When Jesus had finished these parables, he left that place.

The people of Jesus' time would have been familiar with the type of net to which Jesus referred. The bottom edge of the net was weighted so that it would sink. One end was either tied to a stake on shore while a single boat dragged the other end in an arc through the water, or it was spread and dragged between two boats. Fishing in this way meant that the catch included all types of fish—those that were edible and those that were considered unclean. The fishermen had to sort the fish accordingly, putting the edible fish in one pile and the unclean ones in a separate pile. The edible ones were sold and the others were destroyed.

Having a catch that included every kind of fish was "probably the point of the parable. The kingdom draws into itself people of very different motives, attitudes, cultures, and moral attainments, and those who spread its net dare not draw too many distinctions. Jesus, unlike the Pharisees of his time, had no interest in forming a pure church composed only of the perfect. God, in his good time, will judge" (ibid, page 421).

Jesus used all of these parables to help his followers, then and now, to remember that we need to be seeking the kingdom of heaven. We should be looking for that treasure, sacrificing things of this world so that we can attain that treasure. If we wait too long, we may become caught in the net and tossed aside, unable to make the choice we had intended.

Then Jesus told the disciples that the kingdom of heaven was like someone who brought out of his treasure both new and old things. This saying seems to be so different from the others that making sense of it is difficult. But perhaps it is Jesus' way of telling us that worthy treasures can be are both old and new. There were worthy treasures in the history of the people, but that is not the only place

---

How effectively can you relate to the image of the fish? What does it say to you?

What gives the kingdom of heaven discussion a sense of urgency?

What are some old and new treasures that are part of the kingdom of heaven?

where great treasures existed. There were also great treasures in the things that Jesus was doing, in the things the disciples would do, and in the things that people in our modern world will do. Combined, those treasures are part of the kingdom of heaven toward which we are working.

In the Rear View

This lesson has focused on six of Jesus' kingdom of heaven sayings in Matthew's Gospel. The first two seem to suggest something grand about the kingdom and its potential to be more than it at first seems. The second two suggest that the kingdom is worth whatever sacrifices we need to make. The fifth saying warns us to pay attention so that we won't waste time in deciding whether or not to be part of this kingdom. The sixth saying teaches that old and new treasures together make up the kingdom. These sayings provide a wide range of ways to talk about the God's kingdom. Along with scripture and many other words of Jesus, these sayings help us to begin to picture what that kingdom will be like—but still the vision is hazy.

Perhaps even Jesus had a hard time explaining the kingdom to humans. But as we work toward it, the focus will become a little clearer until God finally reveals the true nature of the kingdom to all creation.

After having considered these saying about the kingdom of heaven, how has your understanding of it changed?

Travel Log

Day 1:

This lesson began with a story from the film City Slickers. In that story, the gruff old cowhand taught the younger city man that life is about one thing.

Reflect for a few moments about what that one thing is in your life. Make some notes as to why you identified that one thing and/or perhaps write about how hard it is to balance all the things that are supposed to be important.

Day 2:

Jesus compared the kingdom of heaven to a mustard seed that grows into a great tree. However, mustard is a substantial shrub, but not a large tree. Why do you think Jesus chose the mustard seed as an example rather than a great and mighty tree? What does the mustard seed mean for your faith life? Write a poem or even a few words in response to these questions.

Day 3:

The use of yeast in the second story reminds us that something we might not even see can make a big difference in the result. Yeast, which wouldn't have been noticed once it was mixed into the flour, changes the very nature of bread.

List some things in your life, whether good or bad, that might go unnoticed but that make a big difference in the way you live your life.

Day 4:

Apparently the man plowing the field in Matthew 13:44 was not looking for something extraordinary, but when he found it, it changed his life. Write about a time that you came across something unexpected that made a big impact on your life.

Day 5:

The merchant had been searching high and low for fine pearls. When he found one of exceptional quality, he was willing to give up everything else to get it. For what are you searching? What are you willing to give up to have it? Journal your thoughts in the space below.

Day 6:

Jesus warned his disciples that when the kingdom of heaven comes in its fullness, the angels will sort God's people much like fishermen sort good and bad fish. What does this image mean to you? Does it disturb you? Comfort you? Worry you? Jot down some of your feelings.

Day 7:
Jesus told his disciples that the kingdom was like someone who brought out from his treasure what is new and what is old. We have old treasures in scripture. Perhaps we have new treasures in our own story of Christ's work in our lives.

Take a moment and write about one "old" treasure and one "new" treasure in your experience of the kingdom of heaven.

www.ingramcontent.com/pod-product-compliance
Lightning Source LLC
LaVergne TN
LVHW061342060426
835512LV00016B/2630